From Dirt to Destiny

BY

C. L. GRAY

PITTSBURGH, PENNSYLVANIA 15222

All Rights Reserved
Copyright © 2009 by C.L. Gray
No part of this book may be reproduced or transmitted
in any form or by any means, electronic or mechanical,
including photocopying, recording, or by any information
storage and retrieval system without permission in
writing from the author.

ISBN: 978-1-4349-9682-4
Printed in the United States of America

First Printing

For more information or to order additional books, please contact:
RoseDog Books
701 Smithfield Street
Pittsburgh, Pennsylvania 15222
U.S.A.
1-800-834-1803
www.rosedogbookstore.com

My Motivation...

> "To the ones who love and encourage me. They are the ones that God has placed in my pathway."

D-E-S-T-I-N-Y is defined as a predetermined state or outcome. It implies something foreordained and often suggests a great or noble end.

First and foremost, *thank You God* for this vision that has been both manifested and birthed within my life.

Then to my family and friends, thank you for standing by me. Even when you did not understand that I was leaning on my exceptionally strong faith in God to get me through. *For no one else could have done that for me.*

May my life's journey be a solemn testimony in someone else's life, which may experience some of the same tribulations along life's wide pathway.

To my husband Jerry, *thank you baby* for hanging in there with me.

Then to my children Javier, Christian, Justin, and Jessica, remember to *always* keep your heads up. Just make God and your parents proud in whatever your accomplishments are in life.

To Mommie, just continue to stay strong because *God is still in control* and He loves you dearly. You are definitely not alone.

Then to my mother, Rose, you sacrificed your *entire* life to love God and each of us without measure. Over the years I have definitely tried to return the favor. Just know that you *are* and *always will* be my backbone. *I owe you* so very much.

To my cousin, La Brenda, thank you for staying in front of God on my behalf. Even when you wanted to give up on me, for some reason you could not, and for that you are *truly blessed!*

To my sisters, Ridawna, Corian, Tiffany, and *play sista'* Malia. We may not always get along, but I know that you have my back when I need you, and *ya know I have yours as well.*

To the original *Granny*, Virginia, Jeff, Regina, and Wayne, thanks for adopting me into your family, even when I showed *all* of my true colors. *SMILE!*

To *all* of my nieces and nephews, I love each and every one of you in a very special way.

To all of my loving uncles, aunts, and numerous cousins, I am still going to tell you what you do not always want to hear.

To all of you, thank you for loving me, in spite of, and please forgive me if I have offended. This *was* my healing.

Then, to the Edwards family, and Kevin L.; you all are my extended family also.

To Pastor and Sister, James Brown, who said that I could be anything that I wanted to be, and encouraged me not to ever *sit down on my talent*.

Then, to Pastor and Sister, Wilson D. Douglas III (*www.vlccleaguecity.org*), who inspired me to actually know, that *with God*, the *sky truly IS the limit*.

To *all* of my amazing friends, Theresa Davis-Crutchfield, Clifton Davis, Joyce Benner, Janann Deshane, Brenda K. Johnson, and my other Southwest Airlines (*HRC*) coworkers. Thank you for motivating me to write as you have.

Then to some really wonderful individuals who have once crossed my pathway, and never knew just how much they really inspired me, Andre' Caine, and Eddie Chapman. You were some really great *gentlemen* back then, and for that I am most appreciative. Both of you are truly some *awesome* individuals, who deserve the *very best* that life has to offer.

Also, many thanks to Mr. Danny Kortz, who helped me to illustrate my first book, *Patricia*, written about my beautiful white cat, when we were just ten years old. It was never published, but even when we reached high school, you would inquire about it. You never forgot! You were an enormous inspiration back then, and a really great friend. For that I love you dearly. Thank you, and I pray that your life is right where you want it to be.

Many, many thanks, and may God bless each and every one of you without measure.

With Love, *C. L. Gray*

The Inspiration...

Fourteen years ago, when I lost my closest cousin Dominique, I then understood that tomorrow was not always promised to any of us. I had always heard this in church and was familiar with God's Holy Word. However, I felt that it always pertained to others and not really to me. But this time it really hit home. I definitely expected us to grow old together. Unfortunately that was not in God's plan. That was the first day that I was inspired to write again. Words had always flowed in my head, but this was the very first time that I contemplated putting them to paper again.

Then I lost my very best friend, my father, Butch, who had not always been the greatest. However, he was the very best that he could have been, given his own circumstances. Watching him suffering, yet transitioning into a Christian, helped me to alter my own lifestyle as well. I could feel the Spirit of God progressively elevating me to another level of Christianity and it was utterly amazing. I once told Butch that he had to see me write my first book, and he responded, "Poo, you should have written that book years ago." For a moment I was taken aback. Because I was no longer looking at Butch, but the Holy Spirit within him, which was speaking out through him. Butch was just the bodily vessel used to convey the spiritual message to me that day.

As death continued to take more of my loved ones, including my grandmother, Muddie, and my beautiful sister-in-law, Nitra, I continued to maintain, despite the continuous flow of raindrops in my life. But in all, the love of God still proceeded to prevail and overshadow it all.

Then I lost one of the most irreplaceable jewels in my life, which was my grandfather, Poppie. His loss was so significant that I was taken aback once more. With his passing, only then did I really start to comprehend that I could no longer *sit on my God-given talent*. My life testimony is what I feel God has predestined me to share with others. When Poppie died, I discovered for the first time that I was totally dependent on God, which I had never been before. My grandparents had always been my continued support.

But according to God's Holy Word, "To everything there is a season, and a time to every purpose under the heaven." *Ecclesiastes 3:1*. God had only used Poppie for a season to cultivate, motivate, bless, and encourage me with the wisdom and knowledge to continue the legacy that he had begun so many years ago. Poppie had always recognized my potential, even before I understood it myself. Only now do I fully realize that we are only here for a season.

To my grandfather, Poppie, I pray that I have made you proud of me. I strive to live my life the way that you lived yours before our family and me. You were truly an example of Christian servitude at its best. You gave us our stable foundation and you are the *true inspiration* behind this book. For you were our *earthly rock*. Nevertheless, now that you are gone I realize that Jesus is my *true salvation*. Without your presence though, there is no doubt a great void; however, we must continue on. I really miss your advice and correction. Thank God for allowing you and Mommie to have been such a major factor in our very existence. That stability was the actual key to our success and ultimate survival, and it shall follow me unto the day that I transition over as well. I love you always, *and you too, Uncle Ronnie*. Until we meet again, for I sincerely feel that there is life beyond the grave.

Amen

The Beginning…

As the sunbeams gently prod through the large framed blinds, a gracefully thin, dark-skinned woman bends down to straighten her four-year-old son's collar. Her cattish eyes are illuminated in the midst of the subtle rays, as she leans forward, looking directly into his big hazel-colored gazers as well.

"Now, Butch, Rev. Hearst is coming over today to go fishing with Jr. I want you to be on your best behavior. No-o-o-o swearing, okay?"

Silence momentarily plugs the air, as she repeats herself once again. "Okay Butch?"

"Sure," he replies sarcastically, as his eyes roll up towards the top of his forehead.

Frowning, she calls his name once again. "Butch!"

"Alright, Mama; I won't curse around that damn preacher!"

CHAPTER 1

Born to rather young parents truly unprepared for the tedious tasks of adulthood or parenthood, my dad, Butch, was a wild, drug-addicted, streetwise young man evolving into maturity fashioned much like his rebellious teenaged past.

My paternal grandfather, Papa Bill, was very hard on him, but it still did not seem to deter Butch from the appealing façade that the streets seemed to offer him. It had gotten to a point where Papa Bill would just take Butch around the side of their home to use his fist on him whenever he did anything wrong. For belts no longer did the job and Papa Bill knew this.

However, by the contrast my paternal grandmother, Vanessa, affectionately called "Muddie," was a lot more lenient with Butch's misbehavior. Allowing him temper tantrums, defiance, and mayhem, Muddie tried hard to discipline him. However because of a special compassion for Butch, it overshadowed her parental duty to chasten him as necessary, which later would prove to be one of his very downfalls.

He had been her fourth child, after a thirteen-year gap between the first set of three children, which included my uncles Jr. and William, and Aunt Vicki. Butch actually was the eldest of the second set of children, which included him, uncles Ryan and Lamar, and Aunt Brea.

Because of this age gap, this allowed him just enough access to discover lots of bad habits, such as swearing, drinking, and rebellion. He was also highly intelligent, yet continuously skipped school, and stayed drunk, high, or both, most of the time.

Besides his various insobrieties, Butch also loved horsepower and racing just as his father did. In their quaint little subdivision, a stop sign had been erected at a certain part of the street where Papa Bill burned rubber daily.

Butch had always been the leader of the crowd, but he barely skated through school due to his constant lack of interest in doing what was right. During this time if Butch's curfew was eleven o'clock in the evening, he would come home the next evening at eleven o'clock.

It became quite routine for Muddie to wait by the front door upon his arrival, with one hand extended out for Butch to drop his car keys into her hand. "Turn your keys over right now! Now you're on punishment until I feel like it! Do you understand? Now go to your room!" she would holler out, as Butch's keys fell securely into the palm of her hand.

But what Muddie did not realize though was that Butch always seemed to come up with a new copy of the same car key. So when he got tired of being at home, he would just wait until nightfall to push his car out of the driveway and start it down the street.

Papa Bill got fed up with knocking Butch in the head for the same things over and over again. "Boy, you just don't get it, do you? Come on around the house! I guess it's about that time again! You really must like getting your butt kicked! How many times do your mother and I have to tell you the same thing?" he would inquire.

After getting chastised, Papa Bill would ask Butch, "Now are you going to do it again?" And Butch would cavalierly reply, "Well I'm sorry Daddy, but I can't say that I won't." Then Papa Bill would just shake his head and jokingly tell Muddie, "Vanessa, that boy is humble enough I guess not to lie. But he is definitely a little different. I believe that something is really wrong with him."

Quite the contrast my mother Rose was a year younger than Butch. Highly intelligent, sheltered, and yet inwardly defiant as well, she began to acquire a passionate yearning for all of the wrong types of young men.

As a young child she clung to her father. As he read books in his office, Rose sat alongside his desk with her own set of books.

Her two older brothers and sister, Michael, Jim, and Millicent, called Rose and her dad "Mr. and Mrs. Webster." This was in reference to the vocabulary words in the Webster's Dictionary which Rose and her father discussed all of the time. A house filled with exceptionally intelligent people, vocabulary, religion, and life lessons were a daily topic at their dinner table.

After a serious bout with spinal meningitis at age fourteen, Rose had been left comatose for four days. She still managed to graduate within the top ten percent of her class, despite the doctor's warnings that she would be brain damaged upon the fourth day. Rose had been the president of her junior class, and very well liked by all of her teachers and peers.

Her father, Michael Sr., affectionately called "Poppie," was very hardworking, stern, and demanding of respect. Her mother, Virginia, whom we called "Mommie," was for the most part in agreement with Poppie on all things. So nothing usually slipped past either one of them. However, Mommie was just a little more outgoing, to say the least.

Sadly, despite Rose's good rearing, she could not resist the feral temptation that Butch seemed to offer her.

Rose had attended school with Butch and had seen him on numerous occasions since he had graduated, but really had not given him the *time of day* until now.

The day that Butch came to her house to pick her up, he rang the doorbell wildly, as Mommie came to answer it. As she opened the door, she began to view a drunken fair-skinned teenaged male, barefoot, and requesting to see Rose. His eyes were clearly bloodshot, yet still exposing the crystal hazel beauty in them as well.

"Uh-h-h, is Rose here?"

"Yes, and who are you?"

"I'm Butch, and I came by to pick her up."

"W-e-l-l Rose is only eighteen and normally doesn't get male company, but hold on a minute."

As Poppie walked up towards the open door Mommie, visibly puzzled, questionably called for her youngest child. "Rose!" Now Rose, who was expecting him, walked up grinning from ear to ear.

"Do you know this boy?" Poppie inquired.

"Yes, Daddy, he's here to pick me up for the movies," she exclaimed with an open beam.

"Oh no! You didn't mention this to us beforehand!"

"Well, Daddy, I thought that I could…"

"No, Rose, it doesn't matter what you thought! You are eighteen now, but you still need to let us know these things ahead of time." Poppie interrupted.

"But Daddy? Mama?"

"No! However, he can sit in the front room and visit with you for a little while."

Rose knew that this was the best that she was going to get. So she agreed without hesitation. She was well aware not to challenge Poppie, or his rules; at least not to his face.

That night Butch stayed for a while then left, obviously stumbling out, still inebriated.

Mommie's parents just so happened to stay right next-door, and soon afterward, Mommie received a call from her own mother. "Virginia, I believe that some old tramp is on the side of your house! Sounds like he is throwing his guts up all over the place!"

Now this should have been a precursor to much of the same, as everyone went outside just in time to witness Butch coming from around the house. "Oh-h-h sorry, I had to use the bathroom."

On numerous occasions Butch came to pick Rose up barefoot, high, and even with other women in the car. Carelessly habitual, Butch never ceased to burn rubber off of Poppie's freshly cleaned driveway. It actually became almost as frequent to see Poppie meticulously cleaning his driveway after one of Butch's numerous spinning melees as well.

This seemed very amusing to Butch, but what he did not realize is that it also increased the utter displeasure that they had for him as well. But he really did not care at this time anyway. He and

Rose were a couple now, despite her parents' disappointment and dislike.

CHAPTER 2

Mommie and Poppie knew that she could do much better, but Rose had blinders on for Butch. "You know, Rose, you can do much better than that thug that you have aligned yourself with." Mommie once expressed to her.

As Rose replied, "Well, Mama, he really is a good person. You just have to take the time to get to know him." With this Mommie just frustratingly interrupted with, "Okay, Rose, that boy is going to bring you down, and you are much too smart for that!"

Around this same time, Butch enlisted in the Air Force with his buddies. They were all in hopes of being assigned together, but this did not happen; everyone got separated.

Rose enrolled at the local community college, and for a little while things went rather smoothly, despite Rose's family's varied objections of Butch. But then after Butch finished boot camp, Rose became pregnant.

As their parents found out, Mommie and Poppie thought that Rose could continue her education at the local college and keep the baby without pushing for marriage. "Why drive them together, when we know he's no good for her?" Mommie questioned.

However, Papa Bill, who loved Rose, told Butch, "Well son, since she was good enough to lay down with, she is now good enough to marry." Muddie also agreed, and being rather pressing, told Butch, "Now that this girl is pregnant, you are going to marry her."

So as Butch went away to the base he was stationed at, his parents proceeded to seek permission from Mommie and Poppie to allow him and Rose to be married. They knew that Rose had come from a good family, and both Papa Bill and Muddie were very approving of her for that reason. They, along with Rose, went to talk to Mommie and Poppie to request their permission and matrimonial blessings.

Mommie did consent, but Poppie refused to. He was a prophet in his own rite, and had already recognized the consequences of this blissfully faux union.

"I do not agree to this, Virginia, and I am not going to take part in it at all!"

"Well, Michael, they really do not need our approval anyway, but I am going to go ahead and give my say-so on it. Alright?"

"Do whatever you want, but I am not," Poppie continued on.

He already knew the negative effects it would have on his precious daughter that he loved and adored so much, but he could not stop it. This situation was subtly churning straight "out of his hands" and he had already recognized it. Now a child would be added to the madness also.

Well into her college sophomore year Rose at age nineteen, and Butch at age twenty, fresh out of boot camp, became married. They were finally free to do what they wanted to do and that they did. Still very immature, they continued to drink and party, even as Rose's pregnancy became more and more apparent.

Soon afterwards my eldest sister, Charlen, was born three months premature, weighing in at only one pound four ounces. After Charlen's delivery, Rose happily queried Butch, "What does she look like, Butch?"

Butch obviously overwhelmed and more reserved at the time gently replied, "She's pinkish, full head of hair, and very, very tiny. There's nothing more to say."

"Then why do you look so gloomy? I know that she's preemie, but aren't you proud of our new baby?"

"I am, Rose! But according to Dr. Hasim, if she survives, she will be blind from the high oxygen exposure that she requires to live for the next few months."

"Okay! That's fine. We can deal with that if we have to. She's ours and we will just have to." Rose replied, still oblivious to the seriousness of Charlen's prognosis.

"Rose, Charlen's lungs are not fully developed! He says that she is most likely going to die!"

"Oh no, Butch! Please! That can't be right!" Rose hysterically burst out.

"Yes, Rose, Dr. Hasim is saying that Charlen is going to die!" Butch tearfully interjected, as they sadly embraced.

Birthed into the world to labor just a few short hours, my oldest sister passed away, just as the good doctor had advised. Dying peacefully, yet struggling for every breath, Charlen died the very same day that she was born. Rose never got the chance to see her alive. But sadly Butch did, and throughout the years, he could never seem to shake the constant visions of this tiny precious baby girl from his mind, or from his heart.

"Daddy promises to never forget you, Charlen! I will never forget my beautiful baby girl. For this day will always be etched on my heart!" Butch tearfully swore, as he and Rose painfully looked down at her death certificate.

CHAPTER 3

Since they were still struggling, Charlen was not given a proper burial. Instead they donated her remains to research, which is probably why every August troubled Butch, until the day that he departed this life as well.

Family did not help the matter either, because speculation began to take root as to why this had occurred.

Papa Bill disappointingly asked, "Rose, did that boy do anything to you? Just let me know if he hurt you, and I will take care of him! You know that I will, and he knows it also!"

"No, Papa Bill, it just happened like that, and Butch is taking it really bad as well, so please go easy on him too."

Rose attempted to cope also, as she soon ceased to further her education.

In her quest to show love for Butch she became totally devoted to him and his happiness, despite what Mommie and Poppie, or anyone else thought. Soon afterward, she became pregnant yet again.

But, once again the pregnancy produced no offspring. Instead it only offered more heartache, due to a sudden miscarriage. This incapability to successfully carry a child began to weigh heavily on Rose, as she only strived harder to give Butch a healthy baby.

Once again she became pregnant, and this time she took her pregnancy much more seriously. Rose took every precaution, including eating healthy and taking hormone injections to increase the chances for the baby's survival. She even gave up the nasty habit of smoking, and they were excited once again.

Since Butch was now stationed in Anchorage, Alaska, Rose opted instead to stay close to home. So she remained in Texas, to be close to Dr. Hasim for her high-risk prenatal care.

This also allowed her to stay just as close to Mommie, Poppie, Muddie, Papa Bill, and to the rest of the family as well.

At this time Rose's sister, Millicent was also pregnant, so she and Rose helped each other out. Close in delivery dates, these were really happy times for Mommie and Poppie, as they prepared for the arrival of two grandchildren.

Rose also still spent a great deal of time at Muddie and Papa Bill's house as well. One day while visiting them, Papa Bill and Rose walked out of the house for an afternoon stroll down the street.

"Rose, I know that you and Butch are very pleased about this new baby." Papa Bill happily exclaimed. "Yes, Papa Bill, we are. I just pray that I can hold this one. Charlen was a real test for the both of us!"

"Well you're going to hold this one, and it will be happy and healthy." Papa Bill continued as his smile somewhat diminished. "Rose, I just want you all to be content together. I swear that boy better not mess up! You are the best thing that has ever happened to him, and he knows that."

"Oh he'll be fine, Papa Bill," Rose laughingly said.

"Okay. Because he knows better, and he knows that I will come after him if I have to."

They both shared a chuckle, as they continued to walk up the street.

Unbeknownst to Rose, Papa Bill had already received some really devastating news, which he had only shared with Butch's eldest brother Jr.

Papa Bill already knew at the time that this information would potentially shake up his entire family, and that it did.

CHAPTER 4

Soundly sleeping one July dawn, Butch was awakened to an early morning phone call.

"Butch, baby?"

"Mama?"

"Yes, Butch, this is me."

"Mama, what's wrong?"

"Baby, you need to speak to your commanding officer as soon as possible so that you can come home."

"Why, mama? Why? What's wrong? Are Rose and the baby okay?" Butch exclaimed, as the sheer essence of drowsiness was suddenly strained from him.

"Yes, baby, they are fine."

Silence momentarily plagued the air, as Muddie continued, "Butch, baby, it's your father. It's Bill. He's in the hospital, and he is not doing too well."

"What! Mama, what's wrong?"

"Butch..." she briefly hesitated as she attempted to find the strength to continue to speak. "Baby, he's...he is dying...! Your father, Butch, he has lung cancer! And he's very close to death now!"

"Oh no, mama! No! Mama, no! This just can't be right!"

"Yes, Butch, it is, and you need to come home right away if you ever want to see your dad alive again."

Silent tears flowed uncontrollably down Butch's cheeks, as Muddie subtly said goodbye. As the phone abruptly began to hum in the distance, Butch was left to ponder over all of his mother's words.

With the hours passing, Butch continued to rerun Muddie's saddening expressions as he peered emptily out of the window of the aircraft headed back to Texas.

The evening of his unexpected arrival, Butch quickly burst into the hospital room to see his father. Clearly shaken and overwhelmingly grief-stricken, he cried out hysterically as he saw Papa Bill lying in the hospital bed.

"Daddy! Daddy!"

Papa Bill, barely able to breath, weakly rose and began to scream out to Butch's brothers, "Get him out of here! Get this boy out of here! He can't take this!"

Butch, visibly overcome with sorrow, fell beside his bedside. "Oh, Daddy, why? Why is this happening like this?"

After all, Papa Bill once towered boldly over his sons.

At a thick six foot three inches, Papa Bill always managed to play ball with each of the kids outside and had remained physically fit over the years.

Butch himself about six feet tall and quite lanky in stature had not even reached his father's height.

Now to see Papa Bill, obviously smaller and weaker than normal, hurt to the very core.

As his brothers led Butch out, Papa Bill began to say, "Please watch out for that boy! Watch Butch because he needs someone to look after him!"

He had always known that Butch was the one that required more attention, and he was still continuing to worry about him, even on his deathbed. However, he had to know that Butch loved him too.

Unfortunately, Papa Bill had been a lifetime smoker and that was probably the last time that Butch seen his father alive. Days later Papa Bill succumbed to lung cancer, just mere months shy of the arrival of Butch and Rose's new addition.

He had never shared the secret of his illness with anyone other than Uncle Jr., and not until he was on his deathbed did Muddie even find out. How devastating this had to be on everyone.

Papa Bill's death really agonized Butch, and only drove him further into alcoholism and hard drug usage.

"Butch, baby, you need to snap out of this. You know Papa Bill would not have wanted you to do this to yourself." Rose continuously pleaded with Butch, as he unrelentingly stared blankly out of the window.

Focused on nothing, Butch unremittingly replayed the scene at the hospital, as he mumbled out angrily. "Why daddy, why? Why couldn't you have told us that you were dying? We could have been prepared! Now what do we do without you?"

Even the thoughts of a soon-to-arrive baby could not settle the emptiness and pain that Butch felt inside. His dad was gone. Now at the young age of twenty-two, Butch would have to learn to be a man all by himself. What the Air Force did not teach him, he would then have to discover all on his own, be it good or bad. After all there were no other strong male presences to call upon for advice, guidance, or just to vent to, other than his brothers.

But in that sense Butch was somewhat of a loner anyway. So he knew that at this point, he really had no one to help him out. With that conclusion, he continued to slip into a deeper depression.

"Daddy died worrying about me," Butch began to think, as his heart was besieged with a strong sense of guilt. Papa Bill had died worried about him, but God already had a plan for Butch. It just had to have its own time to manifest.

CHAPTER 5

Rose was just as heartbroken by the news of Papa Bill's death. Nevertheless, she had to remain strong for both her and Butch. She had also been close to him. In fact she had been closer to him than to Muddie. But because of her high-risk pregnancy she did not attend his funeral. Instead she visited with her great-grandmother that day.

"I really need to see Mama Liza today because it's not a guarantee that she is going to be around much longer either." Rose began to think. Mama Liza, who had begun living next door with Mommie's parents, had been asking about Rose for a while. So this would now be a good time to see her.

Well into her nineties, in somewhat failing health, but still very spiritual, Mama Liza graciously welcomed Rose's visit. "Rose is that you? Oh baby, it's so good to see you! I see that you are pregnant once again, huh?"

Gently kissing her forehead, Rose replied, "Yes, Mama Liza, I am trying one more time, and I pray that I will hold onto this one."

"Well, baby, this one will survive! Remember, God is able to do *all* things *but* fail. You already know this, and I have faith in Him that this one *will* live." Mama Liza declared, as she began to pray aloud.

"Heavenly Father, in the name of Jesus, I plead the blood of Your Son, over this baby. Cover this child that no weapons

formed against him or her shall prosper! May this baby's life be used to uplift You Lord, My God, in Jesus' Mighty Name we pray! Amen."

At that very moment, Mama Liza spoke over Rose and her new baby, and from her belief and supplication, *God did not fail her*. This time Rose succeeded in carrying her newborn to term, just five months later. For her, the third attempt was *the gift*. God had finally blessed her with the desires of her heart, and I became Butch and Rose's only living child.

To this day I must praise God for allowing me the opportunity to live and serve Him. Also thank God for my great-great grandmother, Mama Liza, who prayed for me while I was still in the womb.

CHAPTER 6

Butch was still stationed in Anchorage, Alaska, and had returned to his base by this time.

So Mommie, Muddie, and Butch's sister Aunt Brea were at the hospital to assist Rose during her pending delivery.

As Dr. Hasim passed by everyone in the waiting room, apprehensively one inquired, "Dr. Hasim, has the baby arrived yet?"

"No not quite. She is almost there! But I promise you that when I return, you ladies will have a new grandbaby!"

As the room filled with nervous laughter, Muddie and Mommie began to chat again about the new baby. What seemed like hours, but was actually only about a half an hour later, Dr. Hasim happily entered the room to make an announcement.

As everyone jumped up in excitement, he announced, "Ladies, we have a new baby girl! She was born just a few minutes ago. So you should be able to see her in just a little while!"

Smiling and hugging Mommie, Muddie, and Aunt Brea came in to see me just a few moments later.

Out of the sheer pain and anxiety that brisk December early afternoon, I was born into a world truly unprepared for what it had just received. Forenamed after Butch, whose real name was Charles; I became designated as his namesake. Disappointingly though, I arrived just a little darker than my parents, and this came as quite a surprise, because both of my grandfathers, Papa Bill and Poppie, were biracial.

Everyone had been so excited to see the couple's firstborn. Muddie and Brea marveled over me. But Mommie looked on in a bit of astonishment, expecting me to look a lot better. She asked the doctor, "Dr. Hasim, one side of the baby's head seems to be warped. She looks to be somewhat disfigured. Can you tell me why is that?"

"Well you can attribute that to the baby lying on one side, in the womb for a longer period of time than the other," he responded. "Plus she has just gone through the trauma of coming through the birth canal as well," he continued on to say.

Even though the obstetrician was trying his best to explain, Mommie continued to query. She was still very concerned and dissatisfied. Numbed by my appearance, Mommie dully exclaimed to Muddie and Brea, "Well I think that I am going to go ahead and leave now you all."

Hastily Aunt Brea asked her, "Mommie, I thought that you got dropped off? Do you have your car here?"

Mommie quickly responded, "Oh yes, Brea, I-I forgot." "Well did you want us to take you home?" "Yes please."

Now Mommie wasn't the only person that day shocked by my looks either. Rose also seemed a little disappointed. But she still loved her precious baby, because after all it was hers and Butch's. I was his, and that was all that mattered to her. I would finally make the couple complete, so she thought.

During this time Mama Liza continued to get progressively weaker and weaker. The week of my delivery, she constantly requested for Rose to bring me to see her.

For Mama Liza desired to hold the cherished manifestation of her faithful prayers. "I want to see the new baby," she repeatedly stated. Unfortunately, due to the chilly wintry weather, Rose was never able to take me to see her, and Mama Liza died about a week or two later. She was never able to hold or see me, in the natural. Nevertheless, I know that all of her positive words and prayers live on within me.

A couple of weeks later, Rose's sister, Millicent also had her baby. A girl too, named Dominique, born very fair, with the most gorgeous blue eyes, which eventually turned a very distinct greenish-brown. Around that time, Dominique and I both shared the attention of Mommie, Poppie, and our other family members.

Then about three months later, against Mommie and Muddie's tearful protests, I took my first airplane ride to Alaska, to see Butch. The day that we left, Mommie and Poppie were very sad.

"Virginia, did you see the way that the baby kept looking at us?"

"Yes I did, Michael."

"I don't think that she wanted to go." Poppie continued on to say, as they both broke the silence of seeing Rose walking down the jetway entrance.

Looking back at him with a smirk on her face Mommie began to say, "Now you know, Michael, that baby is much too young to understand what's going on!"

"Yeah, I know, but just maybe she did."

"Okay, whatever," Mommie said as they started to laugh and walk away from the gate.

"A long turbulent ride, on a very shaky propeller plane. I won't do that again!" Rose promised as the airplane landed on the runway.

Upon her arrival, Rose was so delighted to see Butch that she could barely hold on to me and everything else that she had in her possession. As we walked into the gate area, Butch immediately met us.

Excitedly he pulled back the mass of pink blankets surrounding me only to state, "Where did you get this little black baby from? Is she really mine?"

Rose quickly responded, "Of course silly! What do you think?"

Unsure that I was actually his child or not, Butch never uttered another word of uncertainty until years later.

Out of Texas, in the freezing climate of Anchorage, Butch and Rose did very well. They remained content and were deeply in love at the time. Although they were still extremely immature, they made many friends, enjoyed living away from their parents, and partied every night.

Rose had vowed to change Butch, yet Alaska is actually where she ultimately surrendered to the pressure and began to smoke marijuana, just as he did. By now Butch had graduated up to intravenous drug usage also. However, Rose would never go that far.

Despite the drugs, Butch and Rose were really good parents. They exposed me to everything though, including all of the swearing, domino games, drinking, and narcotics.

There were also times that Butch would get drunk and go mountain climbing with his buddies, all with me in tow in a backpack. Then there were the various pictures that they took of bears rummaging through the garbage cans at the apartment complex.

We were probably the happiest ever, when we lived in Alaska. At least Butch seemed to be, and that was probably because he still missed Papa Bill immeasurably. This way, he did not have to see Muddie grieving, or face the emptiness of being in the house that Papa Bill had built for his family from the ground up.

During this time Butch also sent for his youngest brother, Ryan, to come and live with us as well. He felt that this would help Muddie out, and give Ryan a chance to deal with the loss of Papa Bill also. Ryan was about sixteen at the time, and he loved me. He played with me all of the time, and he also took me to the daycare for the first time, the day that he returned to Texas.

Uncle Ryan always said that something was *quite different* about me because I crawled backwards. I guess he did not lie. But that would not come for many years to come.

One year and six months later, Butch was honorably discharged. Then we returned to Texas, with Rose pregnant once again, and this is where things commenced to go awry.

CHAPTER 7

My childhood was chaotic, but still content, regardless of the dismay, poverty, and the struggles. It was still contrasted by lots of love and laughter along the way.

Our family was very dysfunctional, yet cheerful, despite all of the turmoil and the varying hardships. It is and was very hard to make sense of it all, but it was the way it was. It was very hard to be the only adult, within a house of four children. These children included an immature father, mother, and a little sister only eighteen months my junior, who still lacked the acquired maturity that I possessed at the time.

My eyes and mind were very wise to all of my surroundings, and even with my short baby stature, I demanded and commanded respect. Since I had been exposed to a vast number of military guys over that past year, I grew up with a very bad mouth, which would swear *at will*. I also tested my *skills* quite often, and in front of anyone who would listen. This included both of my parents, grandparents, and all others alike. It was the ultimate way to demonstrate my frustration, control, and aggression. I was all of these characteristics living within one little being.

Butch and Rose were both very unprepared for parenting, let alone holy matrimony. They continued to party often. In fact neither one knew what either word meant, because parenting came secondary to drugs, and drugs were the open door to *whoredom*.

After my sister was born, Rose began to suffer with post partum, which ultimately nudged her into some larger mental health issues. The doctors soon diagnosed her with paranoid schizophrenia and prescribed her lifetime medications.

Between all of the instances of Rose's personal bouts with schizophrenia, was also a sick idolatry for Butch, and this is where I began to become very frustrated. I had to step up into the role of an adult, even as a child.

Rose was in and out of mental institutions all through my childhood, and it directly affected all of us in one way or another. This included our direct care as well.

When we returned, we began to stay with Butch's aunt, Papa Bill's sister, whom they fondly called "Aunt Kidd." Because Butch's family had been mixed with Creole and Caucasian, Aunt Kidd was a very fair-skinned robust lady, who was also very feisty. She had only recently lost her only son, Brian, and was still struggling deeply with his lost.

But because of our stay there, Aunt Kidd grew very fond of me. She often credited me for saving her from her grief, just from my *talks* with her. Even though I was only about two or three, she always recalled a specific time to me that I had come across her during a period of intense grieving.

During this time, Aunt Kidd was sitting on the couch, in a corner of her dark living room sobbing. As I appeared in the room, she was still filled with lots of sadness and tears.

Simultaneously, as I intensely watched her crying, I said to her, "Don't cry, Tidd. I love you, Tidd," as I gently wiped the tears from her eyes. As a young toddler, I could not say her name correctly, but I did say enough that day to still catch her attention.

Aunt Kidd had not realized it then, but it was only the Holy Spirit working through me that had grabbed her thoughts that day. She had to realize that it was now time to continue on with her life, regardless of her broken heart. For once, I had been *the hope* that she needed in her life, and she had finally paid attention. From that day forth Aunt Kidd began to heal from her grief, as she poured more love into her relationship with me.

Poor Aunt Kidd endured so many fights between Rose and Butch that it was rather unreal. Rose had even burst in while

Butch was using the bathroom, and they began to fight while his pants were still down. It is hilarious now, but I am sure that it was not funny then.

I could hear Aunt Kidd talking to Muddie saying, "Vanessa, Lord they got to fighting in here today, and Butch was naked from the waist down. All I could do is move the baby out of the way, and once Poo was out of the way, I let them have it!" Aunt Kidd always tried to protect me from getting involved, as she attempted to separate Butch and Rose as well, all to no avail.

When we finally did get our own place a few houses down from her, I know that Aunt Kidd was relieved to finally have peace in her house again. She did not have time to grieve with a circus in her house that played out at will.

Not too long after relocating, Rose gave birth to another daughter. My sister Ree was born quite different from me. She had taken after the Caucasian side of either one of my grandfathers. Papa Bill or Poppie, they both had grandfathers of full Anglo descent.

Papa Bill's father was mixed, with a European father and a Creole mother, but he married a very fair-skinned black woman. Poppie's father was also mixed, with a Caucasian father and Indian mother, but he married a very dark-skinned black woman. So Papa Bill had no pigment, with chingy eyes, and skin as fair as a pure Caucasian. Poppie by contrast, had smooth tan skin, beautiful sandy curly hair and high cheekbones that displayed his grandmother's deep Indian heritage.

Because of this gene inheritance, Ree came into the world with very fair skin, light brown hair, and the biggest hazel eyes, that everyone instantly fell in love with. This newly found attention for her suddenly became a menace to me, because of my lack thereof.

Although Mommie and Poppie did not forget about me, I became increasingly jealous and angry about Ree's arrival. Mommie and Poppie still loved and actually wanted to raise me; however everyone else seemed to be in love with Ree. This kept me heated at the world, even though we were just eighteen months apart.

Two months later, Rose had her first mental breakdown.

CHAPTER 8

During this time, life began to drive us like a frenzied roller coaster ride. Butch was back to messing around, and Rose was having difficulty in all areas.

Now between his numerous escapades, Rose's various tirades, mental breakdowns, and all of the drugs in between, Ree and I were very often uprooted to stay with Mommie and Poppie. After a while it all became quite routine to us, and we had not even yet reached school age. Because of these spontaneously repeated shifts in custody, Mommie and Poppie became one of our most profound sources of stability, our foundation to say the least.

As Butch continued to have affairs and get high, Rose continued to do much of the same. When she was sane, she was making herself miserable with Butch, cheating as well, or exposing us to a schizophrenic's abnormal way of daily life. You would actually swear that we were the ones doing acid, or on some type of trip or something.

Did anyone ever tell Rose and Butch, "*Two wrongs don't make a right?*" Someone had to be the bigger person. But again we were dealing with two adolescents who should not have ever been together, let alone have had children of their own at this time. But then again, God allowed it, and God's will *is* perfect.

Seven years into the marriage, as life continued on with the same constants, Butch and Rose began to openly contemplate divorce. Then they separated, which caused us to have to downsize to a smaller house that Rose could afford alone. We had been living in a very nice home. Then we suddenly had to move, and Rose went wild selling everything that we owned.

I can recall Aunt Kidd being there to try and stop the sale of my big toy chest that was made like a large St. Bernard dog. As an older lady inquired about the price, "How much is this big toy chest?"

Aunt Kidd blurted out, "It's not for sale!" But Rose came along and sold it to the lady anyway. That really hurt Aunt Kidd, because she knew that I really liked that chest and the playthings that it held inside.

My toys also had been neatly positioned around our yard for sale as well. Because of her concern for me, Aunt Kidd continued to try to shield my entire collection from being sold right out of my sobbing hands, all to no avail.

That day Rose had another agenda in mind, which proved to be more successful than any attempts that Aunt Kidd or I could have had to stop her. Aunt Kidd had always been able to persuade Rose to do certain things that were beneficial for us, but it became increasingly obvious that Rose was starting to sink again into the grasps of paranoia and fantasy. She could no longer do anything to impede Rose at this point. All she could do is continue to support and stand by helplessly trying to console me, as my belongings were being auctioned off to the highest bidder.

"Don't cry, Poo, everything's going to be all right," she said, as she kneeled down, continuing to stroke my face affectionately and gazing into my eyes. "You know that Aunt Kidd loves you, and I will just have to buy my baby some new toys. Okay?"

"Okay," I sobbingly replied. Somehow I knew that if Aunt Kidd said that it would be all right, then it would be just that... all right. She knew that this was the only way that she could remain in Ree and my life, without offending Rose. So she stayed utterly silent as our things continued to be sold away, as the day proceeded.

In my adolescent mind I continued to wonder, "Where in the hell was Butch, and why didn't he care enough to stop Rose from her madness? And where in the hell was everybody else that could help us out?"

Aunt Kidd could not do it alone. She did not like a lot of things that were going on either, but she really could not comment on them, again if she expected to stay in Ree's and my life.

I was still rather grown and I still had a mind to swear whenever I was frustrated, and this day just happened to be one of those days.

I really loved Aunt Kidd, and I truly appreciated the fact that she did not differ with Rose on this day. She cherished us that much to sacrifice her own thoughts and expressions, just to keep Rose euphoric in her moment of insanity. She knew that if she had said something, that Rose would have instantly told her to leave, and somebody had to be there for us.

I realize that it was all out of love, and we definitely had a lot of people praying for our well being as well. But everybody else seemed to be on the sidelines, while Mommie and Poppie worked tirelessly up front, to continue to help Rose care for herself and for us.

CHAPTER 9

Aunt Kidd could only do so much, but my grandparents really were the ones who struggled through all of the psychosis and the pain. Looking back, this had to be an extremely agonizing feat for her parents to have to watch as their daughter stooped so low.

"Rose had been raised right and exposed to a better life, so why did she have to set her sights on some thug, that helped to change everything about her?" Mommie and Poppie pondered on this question quite often. This period of time proved utterly devastating to me as well.

A very independent five year old now, I heard every argument between my parents, and was involved in every fistfight between the two. With all of the negative exposure, I started to grow increasingly wiser beyond my years. I was more aware than I should have been, given my age.

That year Butch and Rose divorced, and Ree and I were involuntarily thrown back unsupervised into her crazy psychotic lifestyle once again. During this time, Butch went on to revisit various past and present relationships, but always ended up back at our house, and that made me so livid.

Rose was still very attractive and shapely, so she did much of the same, experiencing new relationships also that exposed Ree and I to all types of men. From professionals to the lowest trash that she could find, Rose dated all sorts. She also brought all of them around her young daughters as well. This was very dangerous, but Rose did not seem to comprehend or care about what she was doing back then.

Rose would say, "Okay Poo, you can go on to bed with Ree. I have company now."

Then I would respond, "I am not going to bed until this *SOB* leaves," pointing angrily at the man. Needless to say, the company would soon leave, because I was not budging until they left, no matter what, and these different men already knew it.

I noticed it all and did not like what I was seeing. So I rapidly became Rose's keeper and voluntarily took on the role as head of household as well. I always stayed up until company left to make sure that everything was secure and to lock the door, unless Butch came by to see Rose.

When he would visit, then I knew that I could safely go to bed without worrying. Plus he was not going to take "no" for an answer. He did not care if he lived there or not. I had no choice but to go to bed when he and Rose told me to.

Even though I now resented Butch for his constant absence in our lives, I still hoped for reconciliation between the two of them. I knew that was the only way that I could resign my role as Rose's keeper and give it back to our true head, which was Butch.

Rose was really starting to lose her grasp on reality yet again, which proved to be just as devastating once more. Looking back on it all, I realize that God was the only one that could have protected Ree and I at this rather lowly period in our lives.

Ree spent a great deal of time with Butch's family, and I remained with Rose. Butch's sister, Aunt Brea, and my grandmother, Muddie, would sometimes come to get Ree and they would ask, "Poo, are you coming too?"

My reply was always the same, "No, I am going to stay and take care of Rose." Someone had to be there to watch over her, and I had already assumed and knew my duty, which I took very seriously at every bit of age six.

Besides Ree was the light-skinned one, and I was the darker of the two, so I always felt that I was the least favored anyway. Everyone *oohed* and *awed* over her. I got all of the stares. Because by this time I had a scar between my eyes due to a past bout with chickenpox that I had continuously scratched. It had now given me the appearance of looking almost cross-eyed, which only put me more on the defense and made me angrier on the inside.

My cursing skills had only intensified or become more defined, and I respected no one other than Mommie, Poppie, and Aunt Kidd. That meant that everyone else was fair game, pretty much.

This very well could have been the real reason why everybody liked Ree more than me. But I had experienced the differences that were made between us, and I began to care less about what anyone else thought anyway. I knew that Rose needed me, and I made it my business to stay with her and tried to take care of her as best as I could.

Rose was going through a period of loneliness, despair, and fantasy, and as she went through her various delusional states, she carelessly heaved us through them as well. She would lock us out on the porch from early afternoon until dusk with snacks to eat. Then she would only unlock the door if we begged her to come in to use the bathroom.

Even though I was outside with the other neighborhood kids, entertaining Ree, and keeping her engaged in lots of trouble, my mind would often revert back to Rose. I would always wonder about what she was doing inside of the house.

So from time to time, while we were locked outside, I would get up and just look through the screen to check on her. She would still be sitting in the same dark corner of the room, gazing off into space, in the same position, as each of the other times that I had previously checked on her. I would ask, "Rose? Rose? Rose are you okay?"

Gradually she would snap out of her trance and say, "I'm fine! Just go play!"

Then Ree would get up and mimic me, by asking her the same thing, in the cutest little *squeaky voice*. Then she would say, "Whatcha doing, Rose?" No matter how many times Rose blew her off, Ree would still continuously mimic me and then ask Rose that very same question at the end. She really loved Rose too, but at this time Rose really did not know how to love anyone else other than Butch. She obviously needed help but no one was there to help her. She missed Butch, and he was definitely missing in action.

These times were very difficult and twice as hard to understand. We were all extremely miserable, but no one came to our rescue right away.

CHAPTER 10

There were periods when Ree would beg and plead for Rose to cook food for us, and it would literally take the entire day, for her to snap out of whatever to feed us.

I had just learned to wait until she felt like getting up to cook. But Ree would continue to whine and ask, "Please, Rose, will you fix us something to eat? We're hungry!"

Then Rose would just sit there staring straight into Ree's eyes, saying, "Rose is dead! She's not here! Your mama is dead," as Ree continued to cry and appeal for Rose to stop playing and feed us. She would continue to whimper, as I would sit calmly in the same dark corner, watching it all unfold, looking from her to Rose.

I would sit brainstorming to determine just what kind of help could I offer the situation. Soon enough I decided that someone had to take the initiative to change things around there. The house could not run itself, Rose could not do it by herself, and nobody was coming to rescue us from all of the madness either.

From dusk to dawn, we would just sit in this lonely *shotgun house*, watching only one channel daily on a little 13" inch black and white television. Our sole channel was the public broadcasting channel that showed The Electric Company, Sesame Street, and programs like that. After those shows, I would get depressed, because there was nothing else to watch, or to do at night. I guess it would have been a luxury to have CBS, NBC, or ABC back then. At least there would have been more of a variety than what was offered on this one lone channel.

We would really sometimes sit from morning to nightfall waiting on Rose to get up and do things for us, such as cook, clean, or even talk to us for that matter. She was definitely not the best person to care for us at this time, because she was really in her own world, but she was truly all that we had.

I know that God was watching over us for sure then, because there was no other way to explain why we were able to survive these forced hardships.

It was all too exhausting, living with a schizophrenic mother and her varied mood swings and personalities. While everyone else was going on with his or her lives, we were subtly suffering inside, and in need of someone to supervise Rose and us. But she was all that we had, and that was better than nothing.

Butch had just about gone completely out of the picture, doing his own thing with everyone else, except for us. He would try from time to time, but it was becoming less than normal, and more sporadic than ever. He had even begun to date one of Rose's supposed good friends. Whatever? This person was never a true friend to Rose.

Even I had sense enough to see the signs, and to understand that this lady Wendy was never Rose's friend. Wendy had family next door to us, and her children would come over and tease us about their mother and our father often.

Because of all of the mental anguish that we were quietly sinking into, this did nothing but pour salt on already festering wounds. I fought every day with these kids, and hated Wendy and Butch for all that they were putting us through, due to their own selfishness.

As Ree continued to go with Butch's family, I continued to refuse, because of my duties around the house and my loyalties to Rose. Plus I really got tired of Ree getting all of the attention because of her features, and me getting all of the snippets, just to keep the obvious differences being made *under wraps*.

I really could not blame Ree for all of the one-sidedness though from other family members. After all, it wasn't her fault that she had been blessed with light skin or hazel eyes. Then also, she was starting to become increasingly scared of Rose, and I wasn't that alarmed.

Even though we were experiencing the same kind of lifestyle at home, Ree really could not comprehend the real logic of what was going on around her. Somebody should have explained to her that our mother was *crazy as hell*. But I guess she still would not have understood it anyway, because she was still too young.

Nevertheless, if Ree had not already recognized that something was *quite different* by now, then I figured that maybe she was *slightly touched* herself. Maybe Ree did understand. That is why she took every opportunity to get away from there. This was her *only way out* to keep her own sanity, and I realized this. But I also knew that Rose needed someone to be there for her, so I always stayed behind for that reason.

Maybe I was the real *infidel*, because I continued to subject myself to all of this paranoia. But again, Rose needed someone in her corner, and I made it my business to be that someone. What a wearisome life for a child? I was no more than six or seven at the time, although I still had to run the household. Someone had to do it, and I knew what needed to be done, so it may as well have been me.

I have to give the entire credit to God though for instilling a survival instinct in me, even at a young age. Had I not possessed this inward trait, I would have surely succumbed to this miserable life of darkness and hallucinations.

Soon I began to help Rose more around the house. Likewise I became her closest confidant, psychiatrist, and best friend too. I really got tired of hearing her problems, mainly confessions of love for Butch, who did not seem to care much about what we were going through.

I was young, but I knew that we were quietly suffering, and mostly because of him. He just popped in whenever it was convenient for him, not when it was necessary or pertinent.

In my reckoning, he was just a thorn in our side that came in and messed up the flow whenever things were going right. Butch was no count, and I really felt hatred towards him. However secretly, I think that it was really all just bitter resentment and disappointment, for him not being there when we actually needed him.

CHAPTER 11

Since I could not cook, I started to make lots of sandwiches to feed Rose, Ree, and me.

I would talk to Mommie, Muddie, or whomever else that would call to inquire about us. Even though it seemed as though we were all alone in our own world, my grandmothers did keep tabs on us pretty often.

Nevertheless I no longer worried about who did or did not check up on us anymore. Because with God's help, I had it all under control. I became the only adult in the house and the caregiver.

Mommie would call and ask, "Poo, how is everything going? How's Rose doing?" I would respond with, "Rose is fine, and I just finished making everybody a sandwich, but I haven't gotten to eat yet." Mommie would sometimes hesitate when I said this, and I knew that she would be crying. I would not say anything though, because I had become somewhat immune to the sadness that I felt within.

Muddie would just begin to pray, as she would say, "Girl, I am praying for you."

When I fixed food, I always ate last. I had to make sure that both Rose and Ree ate first. I felt that I had to do this, and it satisfied me to do it this way. That way I could watch them, to ensure that no one went to bed hungry.

Then I would make sure that Rose was taking her psychotropic medicines, and whatever else needed to be done around the house as well. All of this was done without ever compromising my school grades or anything else.

I had inherited a natural capability of analyzing and comprehending schoolwork. So I stayed on the honor roll, despite what was going on at home, and no matter how late I stayed up.

Sometimes at night, Rose would keep me up talking about her problems, even on school nights, until she fell asleep. Then I would be up all by myself, and as mean as I was, I was still very frightened of the dark.

So I began to discover that if she drank milk after her pills, this would counteract the drowsy affect of her medication. Then I would fall asleep before her instead.

Likewise, whenever Rose wanted me to drift off to sleep, she already knew that school was a subject that took me instantly to dreamland. She would smirk saying, "Let's talk about school," and I would snap back, "No, I don't want to talk about school! Let's talk about something else!"

Knowing the outcome of that topic, I felt that I was too smart for Rose to *trick* me into discussing it, since I would be fighting sleep all of the way. But a lot of times, she did outdo me and succeed at the feat of sending me straight into *la-la land*.

As time went on, things seemed to get progressively worse. One day Rose fixed my hair just like hers, and I was so content. It was just she and I together, and she seemed to be so normal that day.

I had quickly begun learning to recognize Rose's good days and bad days, and this one seemed to be a really good day, as she told me, "Oh, don't you look so cute!" I never realized as we were waiting for the cab to come and pick us up, that Rose was in a very delusional state of mind. She continued to beam at me as she stroked my hair saying, "Oh, girl, you look so pretty!"

As we rode in the cab to the store, it really seemed as though Rose was doing much better. When the cabbie stopped in front of the store, she kindly asked him, "Can you please wait on us for a moment?"

As she tightly squeezed my hand, we persistently strolled the aisles of the store, buying nothing. It seemed as though we were searching for something that Rose was not finding, and she was getting quite agitated because of it. We continued to walk, as Rose squeezed my hand much harder. Within her stiff grasp, I began to realize that she was not herself. Then we abruptly left, without her even muttering one word.

Unbeknownst to me, this day she thought that she was preparing me for my wedding day. We were there to meet the groom at the church, which was the store, and he never showed up.

Good thing for me that he did not turn up, or that Rose did not just walk up to someone in the store and perceive that he was that special someone. I may have been in trouble that day, but God's *warring angels* were still protecting me.

Another time we were at Mommie and Poppie's house, and Rose got really upset with Mommie for no reason at all. She suddenly grabbed us up, and left with Ree and me in tow, haphazardly walking through a field of overrun weeds that towered over each of us.

How could I ever forget Mommie's constant appeals for Rose to stop and let us go, as she and the neighbor rode alongside the road? As Rose drug us through, Ree and I both extended our hands out and wailed for Mommie to come and save us.

"Mommie, please come get us? Rose, please let us go? We want to stay! Please?"

As we bawled, Mommie cried out as well. She extended her arm out of the neighbor's car, to gesture for us to come to her, but Rose would not let go.

"Please, Rose, let them go! Please come back! Please!" As we continued to hurry through the field, Mommie continued to scream out for us, with Rose ignoring her every request.

There still wasn't much that Mommie could do. Rose still had enough intelligence to fool the doctors and social workers into believing that we were not in any danger.

CHAPTER 12

Unexpectedly Rose started to cook more around the house. However, she would cook to feed all, including a gathering of stray dogs that had also taken up refuge inside of our house.

She would set the table for the animals and us alike. If we had hamburgers that night, she included all of the condiments on each of our sandwiches, including the dogs' as well. Plates were set for everyone at the table. This became the last straw.

Our house became flea infested, and by this time, Poppie had to come and rescue us all. As he stood on the porch, Poppie shouted out for Rose and us to come out of the house. Anxiously, he would not enter past the threshold. He did not want any fleas to get on him.

As Poppie summoned for Ree and me, he sternly commanded to Rose, "Come on out of there, Rose! Let's go! Leave all of your stuff here and we will get it later."

Rose had been having hallucinations about Mommie. She had even threatened to kill her on occasion, and this time had been no different. But she still had the good sense not to tell Mommie that to her face too.

However by contrast, she still respected Poppie, and was still somewhat intimidated by him, even in her delusional state of mind. Because of this strong desire to please him, she quietly obeyed Poppie's demands to leave our house, and receive the help that she so desperately needed. We were then taken from the house to stay with Mommie and Poppie once again, and Rose was admitted into a mental institution once more, with Butch nowhere in sight, as usual.

Poppie had our house exterminated, and all of the dogs were picked up by animal control. How sad, because these strays had become our friends. They only desired somewhere to live and to be loved. Unfortunately they had picked the wrong house to live in, because Rose had allowed too many of them to stay there. I really loved all animals, so I was a little upset by the dogs having to leave.

But so much was going on with Rose and us at the time that I did not have much time to think of them. Everything was moving all too fast, and we were being shuffled around once more. Having to live with my grandparents yet again, I was really getting tired of these same constants.

The only thing that Ree and I did like about being at Mommie and Poppie's was the time we got to spend with our favorite cousins Dominique, Caleb, and Kendall. Dominique and I were the same age, but whereas I was very rough around the edges, she was more girlish and proper. From a child up, nothing had changed, except for her maturity level.

With their radiant greenish-brown eyes and natural dirty blonde hair, Ree and Dominique always seemed to get all of the attention. Everybody gave it to them, except for Mommie and Poppie, and that is all that I cared about. As long as they both still loved me, I could not care less about anyone else, and that was my irritated viewpoint.

Now Kendall and Caleb were the other equation to our misbehaved mixture. These cousins were brother and sister and they thoroughly entertained us, as they sometimes bickered amongst themselves. It was always funny to see Kendall pretending to touch Caleb, but not actually doing so. Then to hear Caleb whining, "Mom, Kendall is touching me!"

Kendall would then reply, still holding her hand away from Caleb's arm. She was always within a hair's reach of touching him, but still far enough not to do so. With the biggest sneakiest grin on her face, she would say, "No I am not, Mom!" That was the hilarious part of it all, because Kendall would sit and agitate Caleb for as long as he continued to gripe about it.

We had lots of other cousins, but at the time we saw these three the most, and were pretty much raised like sisters and brothers. We really enjoyed our inner circle, until each time that they got ready to go.

They would leave with their parents, worry-free, going back to their nice homes and great lifestyles, while we continued to live with our grandparents. Even though Mommie's and Poppie's house wasn't so bad, it still wasn't home either.

Rose was still in the mental institution, and Butch was still nowhere in sight. Ree and I both got really exhausted with seeing this happen over and over.

Our cousins, aunts, and uncles got to live normally, while we had no real idea what it was like to even have good parents. How could we, when ours were always *missing in action*?

So after everyone would leave, lots of times we got very silent and depressed. Ree would say, "I wish that we could leave too," or "I wish that we had parents like that."

As mean as I was, I never wanted to expose both the disappointment and hurt that I felt on the inside, so I would just respond, "Oh, just shut up and go to bed!"

Mommie and Poppie could not always understand our gloominess after everyone would leave, but they had to know that we were very traumatized by all of these experiences. We felt it more so than they did, because this was our mom, dad, and *ordinary family life* that was ultimately shattered.

Even so, life had to have been painfully agonizing for Mommie and Poppie, because they both adored Rose so much. They also knew the unlimited potential that she had once possessed.

"I can't keep bearing this," Mommie said, as Poppie attempted to play with us on the floor.

"I know, but we have to keep positive for these girls," Poppie replied. "It is very hard for all of us to see Rose in this shape, but what can we do except for to keep praying?"

To have to keep seeing their daughter in this frame of mind had to have been utterly devastating.

CHAPTER 13

Life continued on much of the same pathway for a while, until Rose completed her stay in *the nuthouse*, with the commitment to try to raise us once again.

"Mama and Daddy, I am going to really do it this time. I am going to be here for the girls, and I am going to stay on my medicine too," she exclaimed.

Rose would always do well, Mommie, Poppie, and everyone else said, until she got back with Butch. Then it was downhill once more, and this became the same misguided pattern each time.

In the very beginning, Butch had endured some of Rose's earlier episodes of schizophrenia, and some of the earlier hospitalizations as well, but not anymore. I guess it was easier now for him to just walk away, and let her parents deal with it, and that included dealing with us too.

Butch was only there when Rose was doing well. Now that she was back on track, soon after her recovery, he was back again as well. This time he claimed to be just as committed as Rose was to his family and our preservation.

They remarried just about three years after their divorce and things began to look up for us once again.

Butch had a really great job at a chemical refinery that afforded us a very good life, but the money only brought more access to Rose's and Butch's personal downfall, rather than to assist us in any way. Drugs were still a major part of my parents' lives, and having a little money just made it easier for them to access them.

By this time I was about eight, and I had a very good idea about life and how everything should be, and just how it was not in our household. I now also held a very deep resentment for my father, which would rear its ugly head later on in life.

For a while life was still pretty good. As we entered the eighties, things remained well. That year, we even got everything that we had wanted for Christmas, and then some.

As Butch and Rose brought in our numerous presents, it seemed like a never-ending feat. We were so amazed and seemingly very happy. However, this was merely a façade to cover the ugly reality that still overshadowed their efforts.

They were still on drugs, and that was not going away any time soon. But, Butch still liked to spoil us as much as he could though.

The next year we did not receive anything for Christmas.

But each year, we would still go to Butch's brother William's house for Christmas Eve to celebrate. We would constantly watch as my uncle's family would open a vast amount of toys and such.

Since a couple of my cousins were older, they would give trips and all sorts of other things to each other as presents. This Christmas had been no different.

We had gone to the usual event broke and disgusted, with no presents, only sadness and dismay. As I reminisce on these days, I don't even understand, "Why did we have to go to this annual party, because it really was not for us?"

I really never understood why did we subject ourselves to this kind of torture? It was very hard to view everyone else's holiday bliss when we had none for ourselves. Even though I did enjoy my time with my other cousins on Butch's side too, I really enjoyed the time that we spent together as a family more. We had been shortchanged for so many years on and off, that we never had much of it. So I never took our family time for granted.

After all, my parents could have done the same thing at Christmastime, but drugs took precedence over everything in our household. That included all of the necessities, such as food, utilities, rent, and so forth.

But nevertheless, Butch always dragged us there anyway. After this party though, Butch felt very belittled and depressed. In their possession, Rose and Butch had only about twenty dollars between the two of them.

As we drove home, Butch turned toward Ree and I and told us, "Girls, me and your mama both apologize for not having anything to give to you all. We really wanted you all to have some nice gifts, but your daddy just couldn't make things work out that way this time."

We both responded with, "It's okay Butch, we understand and we are fine." We were very angry and hurt, but we did not want to hurt Butch's feelings any more than they already were. He was visibly hurting just like we were, so why continue to beat up on him?

Rose seemed to be *half in* and *half out of* it. I could not tell what she was thinking because she stayed silent for most of the drive. Maybe she was silently upset as well.

Then Butch asked, "Look, I only have about twenty dollars in my pocket. I really want to get *a set* with it. I need it right now, and I am asking you all do you mind if I use this money to get one? I know that I didn't get you all anything for Christmas but I really need this. Is it okay if I do this?"

He was asking if he could take this last twenty dollars to score some heroin, because he was depressed. Wow, could our lives get any lower?

Well Ree, Rose, and me all agreed that it was okay to do it to make him feel better. "Yeah, Butch, that's fine," we all announced almost simultaneously.

This was honestly the only time that I did hear Rose speak during the entire drive home. She seemed to have been just as fed up as we were at this point, but it was not going to change anything between the two of them. At least that is what we thought.

In some really sick way, I felt like this would keep Butch from being despondent. So if this made him content, why stand in the way of his euphoria? When Butch was happy, we were all happy.

Not that he was so violent or anything, but because he lived a daily life of hurt and hopelessness, and in some sick way, I wanted his soul to be cheerful as well. We were all victims, but just could not see it or understand it. How sad could this have been?

As time went on, Rose and Butch started to descend deeper into drugs. Butch was shooting heroin intravenously, and Rose was smoking as much marijuana as she could afford, and we were exposed to it all.

We got weary of the heavy traffic coming in and out of the house. Seeing spoons hinted with left over traces of heroin laid on the bathroom countertop with small amounts of blood spatter was a constant.

"Rose, will you please tell Butch to stop doing this stuff in our house! He's shooting up all over the place!" I would angrily say. Then I would continue fussing. "Man, it's mess all over the bathroom, and we have to use it too! This is really getting old!"

Rose would not say anything, but my eleven-year-old frame was getting seriously drained with it. These daily drug happenings were slowly causing *the old cursing demon* within me, to rear its ugly head once again.

CHAPTER 14

Rose was actually doing better in parenting, but Butch was starting to return to his old evils. He was still working at the chemical refinery, making good money, and buying nice things. But now he also had new relationships on the side as well. As they say "more money, more problems, bigger money, bigger devils," but that all depends on the person too. Even though we had some finances, we were still lacking at times due to the constants that were around us.

Butch's other relationships also did not seem to be going away either, especially the latest one. Rose knew about them as well, because Butch would always seem to admit them to her and vow to do better. He would say, "Rose, I do love you, but I love her too." This time he was proclaiming an infatuation for a woman by the name of Stella. "Rose, I still love you, but I am in love with Stella too. I'm trying to be faithful, but it's really hard right now. Please help me to get past this?"

Rose was trying to understand Butch's predicament and to be tolerant with him, but her patience was wearing very thin.

"Now what kind of mess is this?" I kept on wondering. At the time I really thought that Butch was *crazy* for telling Rose this. But it also became my same weakness later on in life as well, for I could never *hold water*.

They really tried working through all of their problems, but Butch's adulterous escapades began taking precedence over us all over again. I started to experience all of this firsthand, which began to bring back all of the same resentment for him once more. I also became very familiar with the names of other women that Butch engaged himself with.

Because of Rose's constant tirades about them, there were constant fights, cuts, bruises, even broken noses between the two of them. The police were a thing of constant viewing at our house, for one reason or another.

Even though Rose was doing some of the same things under cover, there was a code of silence between her and Butch about them. This allowed them to sneak by us until later on in life; however, Butch never talked down about Rose. This was very noble of him not to, because he knew all of what was going on with her as well. Rose was doing some of the same things, but just not as candidly as he was.

One dawning morning, Butch came in from one of his many rendezvous with Stella after about three days of absence, only to be greeted by Rose and the butt of her .357 magnum. He entered the bedroom very casually, as Rose began to swear at him screaming, "Where in the hell have you been for the past few days?"

Butch responded simply, "Out!" Then Rose began fussing and cursing again, only to view Butch nonchalantly change into his pajamas and get into the bed as though nothing was going on. Rose was not having that, as she exclaimed, "Oh no, you are not going to bed just like that!"

Gun in tow, she raised the .357 up abruptly to Butch's eye level, as Ree and I ran out of the front door screaming and crying in horror. Barely six o'clock in the morning, and we were both running outside, to get away from the most assured gun blast that was anticipated at any minute.

Ree and I stayed out for a while with our ears covered, backs hunched, and eyes squinted, as we awaited the sound of Rose certainly taking Butch's life that morning. But by the grace of God, that expected gunshot never occurred.

After a while, we started to feel that Rose was not going to hurt Butch now, so we returned to the house as she continued yelling at him.

I don't know who was more scared, Butch or us, because Rose was still not very mentally stable at this time. But she did have enough sanity not to shoot Butch that morning. She had bluffed him, as he lay in bed with a nervous smirk on his face. Still arguing, Rose lowered the gun from his face. Even though Butch's eyes were closed, they were still very jittery. He seemed very frightened or really concentrating on keeping his eyelids shut. As Rose turned away to put the gun up, Butch's eyes followed her intensely. He had survived her bluff, but not too long after this occurrence though, Butch made sure that Rose's gun came up missing for good.

CHAPTER 15

I was already familiar with Butch and Rose's drug usage. However, we also had the constant drug parties. These gatherings were held with acquaintances that seemed to be pretty shady, but were of much intrigue to me.

Looking back on these times, these were some really dangerous situations for all of us to have been in. But I still enjoyed seeing my parents *cheery*, even if it involved them getting high to attain their jubilation.

I was always right in the middle of all of the swearing, the marijuana, the domino games, the card playing, the fights that broke out, and all of the adult conversations. I learned all of their thug friends' names, and could figure out which ones were good, or up to no good. Everyone always said that I was grown. But after all, this was our complimentary entertainment, and I took full advantage of it.

The saddest part about it though, was normally after one of these amusing nights, our possessions were the ones that usually fell victim to all of the bickering between guests. They would fight and destroy everything that we had paid for and then go home. This left everything behind for us to clean up. We kind of grew accustomed to picking up the broken pieces behind them.

It also became very common to see Rose coming in with the .357 magnum to clear the house. Ree and I were even summoned sometimes to go get it. "Poo or Ree, go get the gun out of the chest for me," Butch or Rose would say.

This was all part of our *normalcy*, if you will.

After it was all over though, we would always laugh about the happenings that had just unfolded around us. "Man, did you see that? That was some really crazy stuff! They don't need to come over no more!" Butch would jokingly add.

Butch and Rose were still quite childish themselves. In their late twenties, early thirties, they were still quite oblivious to what life really should have been about.

It is quite amazing that we were even able to arise from this, without it affecting us more than it did. We were *very strange* or just *really dysfunctional*, but again Butch and Rose were still pretty young and immature. That was the biggest issue, but we still had a good time growing up for the most part.

After a few years, Rose could no longer take the loneliness, or the abandonment. Butch had his own life, his own agenda, and it no longer included us, only his new girlfriend Stella, whom he saw as often as possible.

As he would spend his whole Saturday morning washing and waxing his cars, it became a common sight at the gentle dusk, to see that shiny two-toned, camel-brown, new Monte Carlo leaving off of our street, with the T-tops off.

It was either that or Butch's *tricked out* '67 black Dodge Charger, with the big chrome wheels, burning rubber off of the street to go on one of his many escapades.

As he left, it always felt like our hope was suddenly gone as well, because we were always the ones who were left behind.

Rose was subtly losing reality, back to a very distant world of schizophrenia and fantasy. It was all too much to constantly bear from Butch, now that she had become fully committed to her marriage.

Then on top of this, he had lost his job at the chemical refinery because he could not stay sober long enough to be at work consistently. Butch was really testing Rose's patience. He was deeply off into his own world for the time being.

Rose was still very beautiful and deserved so much better than he was giving to her at this time, but she was still allowing Butch to continuously bring her down.

Despite Mommie and Poppie always being there for her, all of our immediate family, which included Butch, Ree, and I, had started to leave Rose behind more often.

Ree and I wanted to be at the skating rink every weekend, and we wanted to spend the night away from home anytime we could. We were typical children at this point, and we were not very happy there any longer either.

But I can often hear Rose's words haunting me throughout the years, when she asked of us one night, "Please, you all, don't leave me! Stay with me! I need you all here with me!"

CHAPTER 16

We were going to spend the night with Butch's brother, Uncle Ryan, and his wife, Aunt Jayne, who was the coolest. After all we were only ten and twelve, just mere children, but we were really all that Rose had. That night, instead of staying with her, we responded, "We'll be back. We'll be back in a few days." But this was not good enough, because Rose needed us to be with her right then. We just did not understand the full magnitude of it all, but she should have told us, "No, you cannot go!" Then it would have been over with. Yes, we may have been mad at her, *but* we were still her kids, and she did have the final *say so*.

Instead she allowed us to leave her all alone. How sad. Butch, Ree, and I, all of us abandoned Rose that evening. The one time that she needed us most, and we were nowhere to be found.

This must have been one of the worst nights of her life, because once we all returned she totally *flipped the script* on us. That evening became one of the most regretful days that I have endured in my life. Ordinarily I would stay behind to keep her company at all times, but I too left her all alone.

When Uncle Ryan brought us home a few days later, Rose was in the process of leaving. She stated, "Well you all left me and now I am leaving you all too."

Ree began to cry and beg, "Please, Rose, don't leave us! Please, please don't leave us! We'll be good! We'll stay with you from now on! Please just don't leave us!" For a moment it seemed as though Ree had successfully persuaded Rose to stay, as she seemed to contemplate on what Ree was asking of her. But then she said plainly, "No, I am going to go ahead and leave. I am tired of everything, and I really need to get away."

After that, I interrupted Ree's constant appeals and asked her to stay a few times myself, thinking that it may *seal the deal*, all to no avail. Then I became enraged and told her, "Well leave then! Just go on and do it! Stop teasing us and do what you want to do! You haven't been a good mother to us anyway!"

And with that comment she did abandon us, right after selling all of our expensive furniture and possessions to a resell shop for mere pennies on the dollar. She waited until that evening to leave us. But she still left.

Butch had been gone for days with his other woman Stella, so we were really alone and quite unsure of what to do next.

As I sat meditating on what to do next, Uncle Ryan suddenly rang the doorbell. He came into the house visually searching the entire room, as his eyes fell upon Ree sobbing on the couch.

Evidently, he had already seen Rose somewhere down the street and had already been advised of what was taking place, because he came in immediately asking, "Poo, where is everyone at? Who's here with you all?"

Before Ree could speak I said, "Rose is here. She's in the bedroom sleeping." Then Ree added, "No she's not, Ryan. She left us!"

"No she didn't," I said. Abruptly, Ryan started into the bedroom, as I attempted to shield the door, to keep him from entering. "I told you she was sleeping!" I screamed.

As Ryan made his way into the bedroom, he viewed what we had already known; that it was just an empty room, and Rose had been long gone. Then Ryan inquired, "Poo, where is Rose?"

It was too late to lie again, since he had already discovered the obvious. I replied, "She's gone okay!"

"Why did you lie to me, Poo?"

"Because we are going to be okay! Just leave us alone! Rose may come back!" I shouted.

Then Ryan said, "You all, go get your stuff. You are coming home with me!"

We grabbed a few belongings and locked the door behind us, never to return back to the place that we had once called home.

A few days later Butch came to Ryan's to get us. He had cleaned out the house and taken all of our toys and things to Grandma Muddie's. Then he burned everything else that Rose had left behind in the ditch out front. This included her clothes, pictures, record albums, and other memoirs. I saw the debris for myself a few days later when I secretly rode my bicycle by there.

Butch was so cold, despite his transgressions that I could not believe it. Even though we were living with him for the moment at Muddie's house, secretly I hated him even more than I ever had before.

These were some of the gloomiest days of my young life. I had been through all of the hallucinations, fantasy, reality, drugs, and schizophrenia, however this was the most traumatic experience. Nothing before this held any comparison to my mother walking out on us.

I hated Butch because I felt that he was the sole cause of it, and since then, only God has been able to expunge the pain of this time from my heart.

CHAPTER 17

As Butch attempted to keep us at Muddie's house, soon Children's Services *caught wind* of our situation, and a caseworker was dispatched to interview us. The caseworker named Mr. Pascal asked Ree and me different questions that we reluctantly answered. After all there was nothing to hide. Butch was doing the best that he could do for us, with the meager resources that he had. We knew that Muddie was growing weary of us, but she was trying her best to help as well.

After he was gone Ree said, "Poo, I hope that we don't have to get adopted."

I replied, "Look stop worrying about it! We'll be fine. Okay?"

"But what if we get adopted out?"

"Why do you keep saying that, Ree. Shut up, we will be fine!"

"But what if we get…"

"Look girl, if we get adopted out, you know my name and I know yours! Don't you? So we can look each other up when we get older. Okay?" I interrupted her and said.

"Okay," Ree said whining some.

"Anyway, you're bright-skinned and pretty! So you will probably find a home fast! I'll probably have to sit up in foster care for a long time, because I am ugly. Huh!" I frustratingly responded with my thumb stuck in my mouth.

A couple of weeks after our family interview, Mr. Pascal was back at Muddie's house. "Hello, Mr. Pascal, how's it going?" Butch inquired.

"I'm doing fine, however, I have some news for you."

"What kind of news?"

"Well sir, my supervisor and I have decided that the girls will benefit in another home. Their maternal grandparents have agreed to keep them, if you will allow them to. If not, then we *will* have to place them in foster care."

"Why is that?" Butch questioned with alarm.

"Well at this point their maternal grandparents are in a better financial shape than you are to keep them, seeing that you are now unemployed. So it's your choice. But we will need the girls to be delivered to their grandparents within a few days, if that is okay."

"I guess I have no other choice, because I will not see my children in foster care."

"Okay, I will advise their grandparents then. Thank you." Mr. Pascal announced as he turned to shake Butch's hand and walk out of Muddie's house.

"Wow, just like that Mama." Butch said to Muddie as Mr. Pascal drove away.

"Sorry, Butch, but you know they will still be in good hands with Mommie and Poppie." Muddie exclaimed.

"I realize that, but I wanted my girls, Mama! I wanted to at least try to keep them. But they will be better off I guess." Butch sighed as he called for us.

"Poo and Ree, come here."

"What, Butch?" We both queried, as we entered the front room.

"Well girls, it seems like you all are going to Mommie's and Poppie's to live."

"Why?" I asked.

"Because Mr. Pascal has just given me an ultimatum to either give you all up to them or to foster care, and I was not allowing you all to be put in the system."

"No, Butch! We want to stay with you!" We both shouted out as we began to cry.

Not that Mommie's and Poppie's house was so bad, but our family had already been torn apart.

There was still hope that Rose would and could return, and then things would go back to normal. If we were to leave then she may not come back home right away.

"Butch, do we have to go?"

"Yes. Sorry, girls, I tried! But I will get another job and get myself straight. Then I will get you all back. Okay? I promise!"

As we left out of the front room very angry over the news, Ree said to me, "Poo, I don't want to go."

I responded, "Well just shut up, because we have no choice! We have to go! Rose will be back for us though, so stop that damn crying!" Even though I was just as sad, I could never show my true feelings in front of Ree. Someone had to appear stronger, even if it was just a cover up.

A few days later we were back with Mommie and Poppie again. This had to have been about the fifth or sixth time in our short lives that we had gone to stay with our grandparents. We had always gone there when Rose was hospitalized with schizophrenia, so we understood that it would only be for a short period until she recovered. But this time there was an uncertainty as to just how long we would be there.

Days evolved into months, and months became a year, then another. Sure Rose came to visit from time to time, but mentally and physically she was absent and no longer interested in being held down by her children. For the most part, she walked the streets, residing far from reality, amidst the slums of our small city, and doing an overabundance of drugs.

Butch was also almost nonexistent in our lives, but he would call every now and then. Mommie and Poppie did not restrict him from visiting with us, but for whatever reason he just did not, and Ree and I really could not care less if he did or did not anymore.

He was now devoting most of his time to Stella, drug usage, and racking up as many DWI's (*driving while intoxicated*) as he could. Butch was treading down a path of self-destruction as well, living in constant hopelessness and blame, but still not *manning up* to change things either.

At night as I lay in the comforts of a cozy home, amidst soft sheets, pillows, and blankets, my mind often wrestled with the unvarying thoughts of Rose and Butch.

As the hum of sirens continuously blared in the distance, all I could do was talk to God. Even though Mommie and Poppie were awesome, I always appealed to God to return our parents safely to and for us.

Our grandparents were extremely loving, but still quite firm. Money was generous for whatever we needed or desired, and they spoiled us with it. They bought us all of the fashions that our parents could not. They kept the cabinets overfilled with all of our favorite foods, particularly Froot Loops, faced just like a grocery store shelf. They did it all, and we really treasured them because they cherished us. But they still were not Rose and Butch.

CHAPTER 18

Ree and I shared ample family time with Mommie and Poppie discussing everything from God, church, worldly occurrences, politics, peer pressure, drug awareness, and life in general. We conversed about everything. Poppie wanted us to be aware of it all, and we were in church *at least* five out of seven days a week. For us that was a bit excessive, seeing that we had come from a life of fun, lack, and parental drug addiction.

We had not been in church in forever, but we somehow managed to survive it all. We developed some really strong relationships at church and joined all kinds of organizations. So it became really positive for Ree and me.

As time went on, I began to evolve in all areas including public speaking. One Sunday our pastor had been so disturbed with the way the children were playing around in the balcony area. That morning he called each one of us out to pray aloud. In the face of all of the parishioners, he made each of us pray one by one. I was so petrified and humiliated.

As children went on to complete their prayer, the microphone was suddenly given to me. Even though I had never spoken publicly before, the Holy Spirit swiftly took control from within.

For each time that I had cried silent tears at dark for my mother and father. For the thoughts of being deserted, and residing somewhere other than in my own home with my parents. It all heaved out in one eloquent prayer.

My prayer seemed more in depth than anyone else's. I proceeded to minister out for help and for forgiveness, for my life, for that of my family, and for other's positioned in the congregation. At that moment, it was just God and I.

I didn't even care anymore, and quite frankly I could not worry; because at that moment the Holy Spirit had taken complete control of me, so no one else even mattered.

As I completed my prayer, there were people shouting out in the assembly. Some were crying, and others were giving me accolades for praying such a beautiful prayer.

After church everyone commented on just how excellent the prayer had been. Then I started to receive requests to speak at certain events, and that I did.

Poppie would assist me somewhat, but most of the time I was made to sit in his office with his huge commentaries and bibles, to complete everything myself. He prepared me to achieve my tasks alone, and he was only there to aid me if I needed clarification on anything. I could tell that he was delighted with me, and I tried my best to accomplish what I could to keep him proud.

Even though I was very talented, I had so much of Butch in me, that I was still a clown everywhere else, including in church. Ree and I were always laughing, even in the midst of what was still going on around us with Rose and Butch. Everyone wanted to be around us. Even though we were growing up with stern grandparents, we were still the *life of the party* at church and everywhere else. "Poo and Ree." We were the team that everyone wanted to have. Needless to say, we really evolved during this stay at Mommie and Poppie's.

Totally oblivious to us though, Rose and Butch were starting to pick up the pieces collectively and had begun to date again. They were preparing to regain custody of us, and Mommie and Poppie did not have a problem with that, as long as they were drug free. Even though Mommie and Poppie were cognitive of this, they did not divulge anything to us, so not to give us any *false hope*.

By now I was nearly fourteen and Ree was close behind at twelve. As we approached our second year of living with Mommie and Poppie, things started to become rather shaky.

Poppie came in one morning from the chemical refinery, with a sharp pain in his chest. He had been working twelve-hour shifts overnight, and was to have seven days off consecutively.

He had come in to prepare dinner for us that day, and we loved his cooking. We looked forward to it each time that he was able to do it. However, what we did not realize is that we would never consume the food that filled the air so pleasantly, with its aromatic savor. That night Poppie had a heart attack and almost died.

As we sat awaiting the ambulance, Poppie slipped in and out of consciousness. I can still recall the bulky syringe that the paramedic slid into Poppie's arm that seemed to hoist his vein as it went through.

At this time we were allowed to stay with my best friend for a while, until Poppie recovered.

Poppie stayed in the hospital for nearly a month. This heart attack had really taken its toll on him, but he was still quite resilient. However, despite his recovery, he decided to retire from his job. Poppie realized that he did not want to work all of his life, and he had given just about all of that to provide for his family.

Since Rose had finally started to make progress, we were soon sent back to live with her and Butch.

As I neared my mid-teenaged years, I had always been sheltered at Mommie and Poppie's house.

We really did not get to do as many things as other teens did, if it did not involve church, like parties and such. Regardless of this, we were still accepted, and very well liked amongst our friends.

At this point, I did not want to go back to our parents, and neither did Ree. We enjoyed the normalcy that we had with our grandparents. We liked the rules, because it kept us in line, and we knew that we needed that.

However, it was something that we just had to kind of deal with. This is where the true problems started.

CHAPTER 19

Ever since I could remember, I had a complex about myself. I had always felt inferior to everyone else. I had always struggled with *who I was*. Why did God have to make me so ugly? Why couldn't I be light-skinned? Why couldn't I be like everyone else? Why did my parents have to be on drugs? Why did my mother have to be schizophrenic? Tell me why?

But it was all a part of shaping me. Because of this, I grew up with a lot of fury and self-hatred. The anger masked the hurt that I had always experienced over the differences that were made between Ree and I, by other family members. These constant thoughts kept me very livid, depressed, and feeling very unloved.

The time that we stayed with Mommie and Poppie had been some of the most stable and fun-loving times that we had *ever* had in our lives. Now that we were back with Rose and Butch, we had less rules and more freedom to do whatever we wanted.

Soon afterward, we started to *slack* in church. Even though Mommie and Poppie still endeavored to keep us going, we now had access to a real social life again, and we took full advantage of it. Since Ree and I were no longer living with them, we felt that we could not be made to go anywhere anymore. We were both slipping away from the stable foundation that Mommie and Poppie had tried to instill in us.

I began to venture off more often from Ree to do my own thing. We were no longer *joined at the hip* and could do our own things now. A lot of times she did not even know where I was at, and that became more typical.

I started to sneak out of my bedroom window at all times of the night with my friends and cousins, breaking all of the city curfews. We were stealing our parents' cars and doing all kinds of things that teenagers should not have been doing, but that was no longer stopping me. The rowdiness that had been suppressed for the past few years was now exploding *full throttle*.

Ree and I soon met some older brothers, Conrad and Cody, who seemed to be very interested in us. They were both very popular and could dance very well. Conrad and Cody won a lot of local competitions and they seemed to have had just as much freedom as we did, plus they both had cars too. Conrad and I started to spend more time alone. He soon became the first person that I slept with, but definitely not the only one.

Even though both of us were still uncommitted, Conrad and I continued to *carry on* for months. We just had a certain kind of connection for each other that kept us coming back to one another.

He had even caught me on a few occasions cheating, and I had caught him as well.

He was seventeen and I was fifteen, both anxiously awaiting our winter birthdays, which were only one day apart. I really thought that I *loved* Conrad at this time, but as I continued to develop into puberty, I became *very loose*. Sex became my release from all of the agony that plagued me, and I indulged as often as I could, with *more than just a few*.

CHAPTER 20

My notion was that sex meant love, and I was seeking affection in all of the wrong places. I was constantly fighting my parents, having sex, and rebelling.

I could no longer stomach Rose or Butch at this point, and really could not care what they thought about my behavior. Since they had reconciled, they had become the proud parents of a new baby girl, my little sister CoCo, and life had been going great for them until they began to smoke *crack*.

Maybe my teen revelry had been the basis for it. Who really knew? But these were their new days now, and how could a couple of *crackheads* really tell me what to do? I felt that they no longer had *the right*. But they were still my parents, and they did still care.

At this point, I felt that if anyone showed interest in me that it meant that they cared, and I was going to *engage* in relations with them. How wrong was I to believe such nonsense? The high school principal's office became my *second home*. The principal would continuously say, "Why are you back in here?" Are you trying to do anything with your life, girl?"

I had been an "*A*" honor roll student up until high school. I had even won second place in the junior high school local Scripps-Howard spelling bee. I was now taking advanced-level classes, but school was *no longer my sole focus*.

I lived to get out of school in the afternoons to have sex, mostly with Conrad. I had even begun to experiment with marijuana, just as my girlfriends were doing. Since they were older than I was, I tried it solely because they were doing it too. For some reason though, during my few attempts, I could never get high. That was just by *the grace of God* I guess. And to think, where would I have been, if I had even once been able to attain ecstasy?

As the crisp leaves of fall transformed into winter, Conrad and I continued in our ongoing *relationship*. Our birthdays, soon to arrive, were just a day apart and somehow we already knew just how we would celebrate them.

Soon after, everything came to a turbulent head. Not too many months later I almost *lost my life* in an ongoing feud with another female.

Pat was both older and stockier than me, but I never cared about how much larger or how much older a person was in the past. I was 5'0" and ninety pounds soaking wet, but I never did back down from any fight, whether I was scared or not.

I was very angry and did not really care about anybody, not even myself at times. So this time was no different than any of the others. It had gotten to a point where most of my fights were wins, and nobody really wanted to deal with me. But Pat and I had *rematched* so many times, that I began to lose count. She was definitely not as easy to shake as the rest of them.

This day, I found myself in a place where I was not supposed to be, and Pat entered with the same *gripes* that we had previously been engaged in so many times before. This time though as we started to brawl, Pat pulled out a large butcher knife. As I lost my balance, she pinned me down to stab me. I repeatedly struggled with her to get free, but she had at least a sixty to seventy pound *advantage* over me.

At this point, I started to think that I was going to die, but I did not stop looking her straight in the eyes. I was going to make sure that she would never forget the angry piercing eyes of her victim, if it were indeed my time.

Knife wielding, Pat began to lunge forward, right in the direction of my appendix area. As I began to focus on the huge blade coming down, I began to close my eyes. I turned away in preparation of a painful penetration and for my own anticipated death.

Life scenes abruptly danced in my head of the argument that I had just had with Rose before leaving without her permission. *"Please, God, don't let me die!"* I nervously screamed from within. *"Please, God, don't let me die! I don't want to go to hell!"*

I already knew that I should not have been in this place where I was, but I had openly disobeyed my parents yet again, and now I would suffer the consequences for it. Seconds of anxiety lingered for a moment. But there was never any pain.

As I felt the tension ensuing, I hesitantly opened my eyes to an ensuing commotion. One of my friends Kate had entered the room just in time, and had slammed Pat up against the door by the throat. She was holding Pat's knife by its sharp edge. God had used Kate to come to my rescue. She had pulled the knife right from Pat's hand by the blade, cutting herself in the midst of it all.

At this moment I realized that I was beginning to *go nowhere fast*. Then days later I discovered that I was pregnant, all at the tender age of sixteen. "Man, this can't be happening to me! I have got to change!"

At this point I knew that I had to change my life around for the sake of my baby. I figured that I knew whom I was pregnant from, but when Conrad found out, he *cowardly* left me. Now I was young, angry, hopelessly rebellious, and pregnant.

I swore Ree to secrecy. But that suddenly changed when I made her mad one day. "That's why you're pregnant!" she shouted. "No I am not! You're just lying." I retorted back.

"Yes, you are!" she said with an angry gloat.

"Shut up, Ree! You're just a liar! I am not pregnant!"

I really tried to cover it up, but it was *too late*. Rose had already caught it, as she stepped forward and pressed my stomach curiously inward with one finger. "Oh, you're pregnant?" she asked. "No, she's just lying!" I responded.

"Well, we'll just see about it. I'll take you to the doctor and let him tell me what's going on."

Then I got scared, because I knew that my secret was out. I was prepared to keep my baby, but my family would not allow me to, so I was made to abort.

CHAPTER 21

Rose and Butch were so weak that they had allowed *outside influences* to make this decision for me. I voiced my feelings, all to no avail. After all, this was *my baby*, so did I not have a say in its survival?

I can still see my cousin, Dominique, as we gazed into the mirror, the day before the procedure. We had been looking at just how large I was, when she suddenly turned to me and said, "I would *never* get rid of my child."

Those words and her image have stayed on my heart since that day. I replied, "But I am only sixteen. What can I do about it?"

I felt like running away, but I knew that I could not run. Where would I have gone? I spent an entire day alone at the abortion clinic, mentally and physically sickened by my experiences. I was so empty, so alone, so grief stricken, as I felt the final fluttering of a baby that would soon be dead.

Conrad was nowhere in sight. So I had to endure the mental anguish all by myself. If I could have run away to save my baby's life I would have. But just as I had told Dominique, "Where could I run? Where could I go?" Even though it was my body and my baby, I could not save him or her. I became *a puppet* to a decision that was not even my own.

As the nurse grasped my hand, I could sense the gentle tug of the vacuum, as my baby was torn out of me. Tears streamed down like running faucets from my eyes, as I imagined how my baby must have been feeling right at that moment.

"Did the baby feel any pain? Did he or she feel my emotional trauma as well, as we were parted from each other?" I was overcome with grief and rage, as I had to allow someone to steal my precious baby from me.

My mind then shifted to Conrad and me coming together to create this beautiful life. This was a life that he cared nothing about, and I truly hated him at that moment for it.

The humming seemed endless, as the nurse exchanged gazes with the doctor, and told me, "Hold on, baby. We are going to do this one more time. So just hold on for a minute. It will all be over in a moment."

Looking back on everything, I regret the day that I had to give up my first babies, which turned out to be twins, just like Conrad. That day I wrote him a three-page letter chronicling everything that he had missed out on, and detailing what organs had developed in these babies the day that they were stolen from me.

This was truly one of the most regretful memories of my teenage life. I wanted Conrad to hurt just like I did. He had to feel the loss of his kids, just as I did.

"If I had just been older, or more in control of my own life, things would have been totally different." I began to think. "If only I could have done it all over again, my babies would have still been growing inside of me." I continued to angrily consider.

Pondering over all of these things, depression began to creep upon me once more. That day, I made a conscious decision to change my life for the better.

I would dedicate my life to my babies, and become a mother that they would have been proud to *call their own*.

I became celibate and began to work very hard in school once again. Nevertheless, depending on what weaknesses you are dealing with, *the test* is going to continue to come around. That is until you are finally delivered from it and can truly overcome.

I struggled with promiscuity, lust, and the desire to be loved, and I soon discovered that these traits still lay dormant within, until someone came along to *cultivate* them once again. Even though I had suppressed it well for about a year after the abortion, my *desire* still had not disappeared.

Then I met another person who would ultimately change my way of thinking once more.

Twenty-one year old Steve was so handsome and athletic, and he knew just how to manipulate me into believing everything that he said.

He would tell me, "Oh, baby, I love you. You are going to be my wife!"

I really thought that he cared about me, until he began to hit on me. This had never occurred before. However, I was very *taken* by him. Not even the constant blows made me want to leave him alone.

One day I was at the window admiring the handsome guy that lived next door, when Steve came upon me.

Observing *the neighbor* as he walked by, I thought that he was rather interesting, although he never noticed me watching him.

Then very *unexpectedly*, I felt the stinging force of a fist to the back of my head. "Who in the hell are you looking at out of the window?" Steve furiously queried.

"I was just looking out of the window!" I replied as I rubbed the back of my cranium. Then Steve snatched me back, and looked for himself, just in time to view *the neighbor* walking by.

"You lied to me! I ought to hit you again!" He yelled at me, as I winced back from him. "But I am not going to worry about it. He'll never look at you anyway! Then again, who knows! You'll probably be messing with him next!"

It was all too sad, but actually the beatings and the bruises made me feel like Steve really did love me. He would tell me, "Nobody else will want you! You are ugly, black, and skinny!"

Everything that he could say to tear me down, he did, and I believed his every word. "You have nothing to offer to anyone! You're stupid and poor! Besides, nobody else is going to put up with you like I do!" Everything that he said severed me into little pieces, and that is what he aimed to do.

Ignorantly I thought that I could never find anyone better looking than him to love me, because I was as hideous as he had said. I bought into his constant battering and abuse. I became what he wanted me to be, which was nothing without him.

Silent teardrops would flow down my cheeks, as he stood there taunting and smirking.

Only to exclaim later, "Baby, I love you and I am sorry, but you make me mad sometimes!" Unfortunately I bought into all of this *stuff*, because Steve recognized and thrived on my insecurities, and I could not see past that.

His father had been absent in his life, and I figured that all he needed was love. While I was taking all of the pain, I foolishly thought that I could provide that *if* he would only allow me to. I would tell him, "I still love you, baby, and I am sorry for making you mad," as my head hung low in disgrace and fault.

I had so much physical attraction for Steve that I could not even think in school any longer. My grades began to suffer once again, and I began to see the inside of the school less and less despite Butch and Rose's wishes.

Barely seventeen, I dropped out of school, the second semester of my eleventh grade year. I had been in gifted and talented classes, excelled on written tests, and skilled competitions. I had even achieved in advanced level Spanish courses, but nothing could stop me from quitting school to be with Steve.

I was definitely hurtling toward a life of real poverty and despair, although I could not see it. What a waste of my time!

All of my energy was spent with Steve, and I became pregnant once again at seventeen. This time I refused to get an abortion. This would be my revenge for my other babies that had been so cruelly taken.

"I am going to have this baby and *nobody* is going to take it from me! I'm grown now!" I declared.

I was going through with this pregnancy, and I thoroughly believed that Steve would be there for me.

Nonetheless, I was *sadly mistaken* when instead he moved in with another woman.

He only came by to see me whenever he wanted a *change of scenery*. I became *the toy* that Steve only *pulled out* when he wanted to play with *someone different*. This was not very often, but I anxiously awaited any attention that he gave.

One day he came over and I made an angry comment about him being absent in my and the baby's life. "Steve, you are sorry! I thought that you would be different than Conrad. You're nothing to me or to this child!"

The next thing that I felt was a firm fist right in the middle of my chest, as I doubled over in pain. I gasped hard to catch my breath. "Next time you'll keep your mouth shut!" he said.

Once he had even raised me up off of my feet, by my four-month pregnant stomach and angrily inquired, "Is this my baby, Poo?"

As I wailed out in a sensation of pain, I responded, "Yes, Steve, you know that this is your baby! Why are you doing this to me? Put me down! This hurts! What about the baby?"

As he put me down, he grimaced and said, "It better be mine, or else I am going to beat you again!"

Soon it became just *my baby and I*, as I felt the customary kicks inside my belly, which I cherished wholeheartedly. I would stroke my abdomen, beaming with pride. It seemed so exuberating to feel the instant jerks of a little one within that Steve and I had created. Even though it was all rather bittersweet, because I shamefully grieved for the babies stolen from me with the abortion the year before.

During this time Conrad and I became friends once again. I really think that he bore the same guilt about the abortion as I did, as he requested to touch my stomach one day. Rubbing it apprehensively, Conrad and I began to speak about *the twins* that had been taken from me.

I told him, "For the record, I am sorry for getting rid of your babies. But we were not ready for them. I only wish that I had been allowed to make up my own mind though. That is why I am having this baby, and nobody is going to stop me."

Then he told me, "I understand. Neither one of us was ready to be a parent back then. But now you are doing it all over again. What is up with you?"

As I hit him gently and jokingly, I replied, "Don't worry about it! But you owe me three hundred and fifty dollars for that procedure too!"

We laughed as I announced that Conrad's new nickname would be *Three hundred and fifty*. We finally had become just friends who talked on the phone about what went on in our personal lives and with our companions. We had really started to make up for lost time, even though we were both in love with someone else now. We also discussed sex often, but never engaged in it again together. We just remained *good friends*, the way that it should have been from the beginning.

CHAPTER 22

Six months into my pregnancy, I began to feel some severe cramping. I had always had slight pains, but not like these. I had just come in from hanging out with friends, welcomed to an almost empty house, other than Butch. "Where's everybody at?" I inquired.

"Ree is at Edward's house, and Rose is out somewhere also."

Even though I was agonizing, I did not want Butch to know what was going on, so I attempted to keep calm. I had in my mind to wait on Rose or Ree to come in. I wanted to tell them instead, although I was quietly suffering by then.

I was in such pain that I tried to lie down and go to sleep, but that certainly was not happening either. As I lay down, I felt a sudden urge to use the bathroom. So I got up to go, when I felt something really strange.

As I positioned myself on the toilet, I experienced a sudden burst of pressure amidst massive cramping. Simultaneously I could feel the warm free flow of blood trickling down my legs, as the rest exploded outward and generously polished the toilet bowl. I was horrified as I felt the pressure against my pelvis getting more and more explicit.

Abruptly I rose, as a remnant of blood flow and gushes of clear fluid, streamed freely from me. I could still feel my baby *balling up* in knots in my abdomen as the pain became immeasurable. At this point, I knew that I was in active labor and the baby was possibly in distress.

Even though I did not want to tell Butch, I knew that I needed some assistance for my child. "Butch, I think I am in labor!"

"Aw girl, come on! You've got to be kidding!"

By this time, Ree was walking in, followed by her longtime boyfriend Edward. "Poo, what's wrong?" she was asking me, as I anxiously responded and doubled over in pain.

"I think I am in labor!"

"Oh no, girl!"

In all of the commotion, I vaguely remember anything other than my arrival at the hospital. To be poor, black, and young can really be a disadvantage at times.

As the nurse reacted calmly to my dilemma, I continued to panic as I appealed for her to help my baby.

"Look, we need to get these questions out of the way first!" she scowled. "Now how old are you, and how far along are you?"

"I'm seventeen and I am almost six months pregnant! Now can you help my baby? Oooooh, I'm in pain!"

"Wait just a minute! We have to wait on the doctor! Are you sure that you're not farther along, because there's more water than blood here?"

As she continued to query me, I became more irate in my responses. "Look, I need some help! Just get me some assistance! I'm not saying anything else until somebody can help me!"

The nurse looked at me real funny, but she saw that I was not backing down. Then she left the room summoning the doctor. That was one small victory but still not in enough time.

I remember being rolled down to the operating room as the hospital staff continued to move in somewhat of a *snail's pace*. In my mind I already knew, but I had to remain positive.

Nevertheless, the lack of urgency made it painfully obvious that my precious baby was already gone. Her movements at home were the last ones I would ever feel from her. It would also be the last time that we would ever be physically connected again.

The bright lights of the recovery room blazed luminously overhead as I slowly came to. Cautiously still, I began to collect my thoughts as my hand reflexively patted my abdomen.

The apparent tenderness clued me in on what was suddenly lacking as my mind began to wonder again. "Where was my baby? Had she somehow made it through, and they were just getting her ready to see me?" I was hoping for a miracle that day, but I guess it just was not happening.

No one ever personally came in to tell me anything about what had happened or about her period. I just began to read the various facial expressions as the nurses checked on me.

I figured that there was no need in asking either, because if there were any good news, everyone would have already been congratulating me. Even though I was still too young for a baby.

What did I tell you? Being young and poor really has its disadvantages.

CHAPTER 23

As the doctor made his way readily into the hospital waiting room to speak to my family, Ree and Rose got up very cautiously. As Dr. Foley spoke to them, garbed in scrubs with a hint of blood spatter, he said, "I am very sorry, but we could not save her."

"What do you mean you all could not save her?" Ree blurted.

"Yes, what do you mean, Dr. Foley?" Rose also inquired.

"No, she's fine. You all will be able to see her shortly, but the baby was just too small to save. As a matter of fact the nurse is just coming out now to let you all go back there," the doctor announced as he walked away with a smile.

Looking out into a blank gaze, I turned my head slightly in response to the knock.

"Knock, knock, guess who's here?" Ree and Rose appeared from behind the door apprehensively smiling from ear to ear. I just retreated back to my depressive trance opposite of them facing the wall.

"Are you okay?" Rose inquired, as she attempted to touch my back.

Then Ree walked around to face me as she said, "I am sorry, girl, but they did all that they could."

Somehow I already knew this, but I had been hoping for a miracle ever since being wheeled in from recovery. For the very first time since they had walked into the room, I began to come out of my grief stricken trance, to give Ree my undivided attention.

As I gazed up at her with a noticeable frown, I requested of both of them to just give me some time. "Please why don't you all just go and leave me alone! Just give me some time! I don't want to be bothered!"

"Well we were just trying to be here for you and that's the way you're going to treat us?" Ree angrily scowled.

Just then Rose caught her by the shoulder and told her, "Baby, let's go."

Then she looked my way, tears obviously swelling in her eyes as she told me, "Poo, it's not our fault that you're going through all of this. Nevertheless, we will give you some space. But we are here when you need us, or when you just want to talk. Okay?"

I never replied as they both walked out of the room. Instantly I felt terrible because, after all, I knew that I was wrong. But at this point, I just wanted to crawl up in a deep hole and sleep away the pain uninterrupted. I did not want any company. I just wanted to grieve for the baby that had once happily graced my abdomen and my heart.

"So this is what a miscarriage feels like," I began to think. I had first experienced the heartache of an involuntary abortion. Now I had to endure a miscarriage as well. This was all tremendously devastating to me, to say the least. I agonized over the fact that I had lost yet another baby. This had been the one that nobody was going to stop me from having.

I had already contemplated over a few names. Her chosen name was to be "Tai" *(pronounced Ty)*.

I suddenly angrily wondered, "Why had God allowed this to happen to me again?"

Although, I now realize that it was never supposed to have been. Yet because of my lack of maturity back then, I still did not fully understand why.

There was definitely more to life than Steve or any ties to him. Tai had just happened to be one of those *victims of circumstance* that would have been reluctantly caught up in this abusive scenario. But thankfully she was freed before it was all too late. Again, I was alone once more, and very frustrated with repeatedly being hurt.

I began to think, "Do I really deserve this?" But I had never been faithful to anyone either. Just as my *so-called* boyfriends cheated, I did as well, and it seemed to have been catching up with me. *I was always left holding the bag.*

I had been caught unfaithful on numerous occasions, and really did not care at the time. My philosophy was to do it to them before it was done to me.

I always felt that I was not pretty enough for someone to truly love me, so I really trusted no one and kept finding new conquests along the way just in case. This was supposed to be my insurance to avoid the hurt of being denied due to my darker skin or ugly features. How wrong was I?

But I knew that I was *not an angel*. Nevertheless, I began to wonder, "Did I really deserve the treatment that I was receiving?" I guess it really depends on what lessons you learn from what you constantly go through, and whether or not you strive to change things or not. Even though I aspired to be different, I still continued *to be me*, which included *all of the bad* and *some of the good*.

During these times, Butch and my relationship became very tumultuous. In all of my own chaos, I had no respect for him anymore and he was very agitated with me as well. Both he and Rose were still smoking *crack cocaine* and I really could care less what they thought.

Between his frustrations due to the frequent drug cravings and my own anger built up over the years for him and Rose, Butch and I bumped heads quite often. Anything that he said to me was taken as a *jab*, and I would of course *retaliate* with my mouth.

Once he told me, "I see it's about that time that I get on that head of yours again. Huh?"

Then I replied back to him, "What are you going to do to me? You ain't nothing anyway!"

Then the battle was on, which was really no competition. But it still did not stop me. I belittled and swore at him every chance I received. Then we would fight and Rose would always have to come in to intervene.

"Poo, keep your mouth shut! This is your daddy! You have to listen to him!"

Then I would respond, "Screw him! How do you even know that he is my daddy! We don't look nothing alike!" as Rose would work tirelessly to keep us apart.

Then to Butch she would fuss, "Now you're not going to continue beating on her like a man! Leave her alone!" Then they would get into an argument and I loved it.

I hated Butch being there with us. Especially the times when Rose was not home, because then I had no *ally* to help me when the violence erupted. Most times ended up with me getting up off of the floor or running from the house barefooted to get away from him.

He would then respond, "You aren't even mine anyway! Go find your real daddy!" Then I would always reply, "Screw you and your crippled mama too," referring to Muddie, whom I had started to *disagree with* also.

Back then I sported lots of black eyes, bumps, and bruises for my blatant disrespect. However, it still never stopped me from saying whatever was on my mind, whether wrong or right, good or bad.

My head became immune to the constant heartbreaking blows that it endured at the hands of my father. But none of it still stopped me from being *me*. I had to always have the last word regardless of the repercussions.

"Poo, please keep your mouth closed!" Ree would beg me. But it was never good enough until I got my head bashed in.

Even though I was an angry teen and showed very little respect, I would still find myself laying down on my bed and crying afterwards.

"God, why won't you just let me die? Just let me die in my sleep! Please, just take me out of this miserable life that I am living! I can't take it anymore! Why am I still here?" I would relentlessly cry.

It was almost as if I wanted to be hurt. I felt so low about myself that *in my mind* I needed to be beat. I could not *torture* myself, but I would keep arguing with Butch until he would break. Then *my tongue* became the cause of my self-inflicted pain, and afterward I would *cry* and *snot out* all of my frustrations in my pillow.

It was all very strange, but it seemed to be a form of *self-punishment* to myself for living. For I already knew the dreaded outcome of Butch's and my many *melees*, and that was that I was going to get hit each time that I talked back. But somehow I welcomed every blow.

There were so many occasions where I contemplated suicide, *however* I never had the guts or the heart to go through with it. I was just too fearful to experience the excruciating pain of taking my own life. Even though you would think that I was very numb to any feeling, I was still quite petrified to try *the unknown*. That is the only thing that kept me from ever trying it, which proved to be *a great blessing* for me. Had I thought that suicide would not have been agonizing, I probably would have done it a long time before.

But it would have been the biggest *waste* of life that someone could ever comprehend. *Everyone has a purpose to live!* Nothing is worth taking your life… I mean NOTHING!!!

Everytime that I even prayed to die, God would *always* wake me up to a brand new sunrise upon my face. Even though I would wake up disappointed, He always knew what was better, *and* that is why I am still here today.

Just as God's mercy is renewed in us daily, *trouble does not last always*. What you endure today, you may find that your tomorrow *can change* the circumstances. That is what I am reminded of each time I think about God and *all* of His amazing promises to us.

You just have to be patiently expecting, and take *the time* to hear Him. I have *learned* over and over that we have no other hope other than Him, and that is in the Word. *Read it for yourself!*

CHAPTER 24

After a while, although still through all of these occurrences, I began to pick myself up a bit. I waited about a year and then decided to get my GED. Rose had been begging me to do something before, but it never really *sank in* before then. She would tell me, "Poo, you cannot just sit in the house all day doing nothing! Butch is not going to allow this and neither am I! You have got to go back to school, or your alternative is a GED! You have got to do something! One or the other! But you cannot just sit around here doing nothing!"

Now in all of this, not once did Rose ever compare me to Ree, who was very determined to finish her course. After all, she was a track standout with an assured scholarship, and was also doing very well in her classes.

Ree knew that the odds were against us if we stayed at Rose and Butch's house. She also had been motivated by *the notion* that she did not want to live poorly all of her life. Thereby, the only way to change her circumstances was through education, sheer determination, and lots of hard work, and that is what she did.

Ree would even say, "Girl, you are a dropout! How are you ever going to support yourself living like this? You better get back in school, or you're going to be on welfare all of your life!" I hated to hear her fussing, because she acted like some *old prune* scolding a child, and I had to do it my way.

"Do I really have to hear this mess? I thought that I was the oldest child! I don't need to hear some silly stuff from my *little* sister!" I would rebelliously express.

Then she would come back and say, "Well, if no one can tell you anything, just continue on in your mess! But when I leave for school, don't get mad at me. Because you can do the same thing, but you're just lazy! Poo, you were the one in gifted and talented classes. Now you aren't doing anything with yourself! What a freaking waste!"

All of this irritation became the motivational basis for my achievement, and I know that is what Ree was striving to do all along. Even though I did not want to hear it then.

The day I took my GED, I quickly realized that I was in the wrong place. Not that I was any better than anyone else, but I had too much potential to settle for anything less. "Why was I sitting up testing for an alternative to a regular high school diploma?" I wondered.

I had been scheduled to graduate with honors, but had now sunken so low. My head was still *above water* though, and that is all that counted. I had finally gotten my diploma, which made me proud to say the least.

When I came back into the testing area to discuss my results, the facilitator shocked me as he asked, "Why are you here?"

I did not quite understand what he meant at the time, as I responded rather sarcastically, "I am here to get my test scores. What else?"

However, he quickly told me, "You shouldn't have been here at all. Look at your scores! Your percentages are all above average. Didn't you say that you had not been in school in over a year?"

"Yes, sir, that is all true," I casually replied. "Let me ask you? Your last name is quite familiar. What are your parents first names?"

"Rose and Charles."

"Same last name as yours?"

"Yes."

"Ahh! I see why your scores are above average. Your mother was very smart. She once worked under me as a facilitator here."

"That's nice." I responded still quite nonchalantly.

He had remembered Rose, who had once been employed there before another bout with mental illness in the earlier years.

Everyone that knew Rose had known that she was a *walking talking brain* who just ended up choosing the wrong man to marry. This had been her downfall from grace, and he even knew the story.

"Now that I know who your mother is, I know that you're no dummy! Just get yourself together, and you can still go far. Don't let this stop you from doing something good in your life." He preached on to me, as I casually looked away unaffected by his gentle scolding.

I was the typical teen. Even though I was trying, I still did not care and I definitely did not want to hear anyone else's opinion about *my* life!

I felt like he was just *preaching to the choir* on that, because I was going to *do me*, no matter what. Nevertheless, I came out with my GED, right before my graduating class walked that year.

I was still depressed on commencement night though. I knew that I should have been a part of my fellow graduating class. I never got to wear a cap, gown, or to even walk, and that hurt.

That is why I encourage everyone to *never give up*. Stay in school and enjoy the moment. When it is your time to shine you will be glad that you did. Some people only wish that they had the same opportunity to do it. *I know that I do!* But it is still okay. If a GED is the best that you can do, it is still *quite an accomplishment* either way!

CHAPTER 25

Ever since I could remember I still felt that I was *less than* everyone else. I was very inferior to all of my *lighter-skinned* family. I was the darkest out of both of my sisters and that really bothered me. I was the one with *no talent*, and *a scar* that followed me throughout the first half of my life.

I never felt that I was worthy enough to be content, but God knew better, and He was getting ready to change all of that.

My life had been continuing on, like a spiraling roller coaster. One minute I was up and then I was down again, and everything was moving so fast.

In the past, every person that I had been with, had either used me, or I had not recognized the full potential in him and moved on to *the worst* of what I could find. To the ones that were worth waiting for, and who tried to change me, I do apologize that I did not recognize what was right before me.

But God already had a man *groomed* to suit me, that he was *molding* a thousand miles away. He was created *just for me*.

To God be all of the glory, *for He truly knows* what we need, and when we need it.

Who ever thought it would be the man *right next-door* though? Remember the good-looking neighbor that Steve hit me for looking at?

Everyone wants to find that perfect someone who is going to give unconditional love and compassion, even when we do not love ourselves.

Unfortunately, we sometimes go out seeking adoration in all of the wrong places, when we should really wait on it to come to us.

When God is ready, you *will* find that special person that you were predestined to unite with. That will mean that the time is *just right* for you.

In my case, I met the man of my dreams *right next door*. It is still sometimes hard to believe, but God knew it *all of the time*.

CHAPTER 26

There was something so special about *the neighbor* that I always found him intriguing and very interesting to watch. He was extremely quiet, to himself, and seemed to be rather hardworking.

He never knew just how I watched him from my window. I always wanted to see what he was doing, and to know whenever he was at home. Since he never spoke when I would speak to him, I would roll my eyes at him *often*. It was quite amusing, because he never knew why. Now knowing where he had come from, *I see why* he was not that open for greetings.

Back then I didn't understand why I was so interested in him, but the Holy Spirit was working in me, and subtly bringing this man into my sight. I liked him before he ever knew my name, and before I knew his as well. He was very nice looking and very quiet, and definitely *a person of interest* to me.

One day my cousin, Lisa, came to pick me up for a *little joyriding*, and I came out adorned in a half shirt and miniskirt. *The neighbor* just happened to be on the porch sweeping, and briefly looked up. Then he went back to sweeping.

That made my day so I tried to get some additional attention. This time I made as much of an entrance into the car as I could. As I did, I noticed that he had taken a double take, and that was all that I needed. That made my day, and to this day, he says that he does not even recall it.

That just goes to show that women are *more sensitive* and *sensual* beings than most men. Some men are, but *generally* it is not in their characters to be so.

As time went on, I went on with my life. The family was still *quite dysfunctional*, but happy.

All of our friends loved to gather at our house, and watch our mom and dad joke around. They were still on drugs, but they were *mellower* than they had ever been before.

I was still interested in knowing more about the man next door. Then finally, I was able to talk to him, and this is where it all began.

CHAPTER 27

What was so utterly amazing is that, in our discussion, we found out that we had grown up totally different, yet the same. He had come up in the projects on the south side of Chicago, and I had come from somewhat humble beginnings also.

My parents went through circumstances, and his parents did as well. His father, now deceased, was very strict on him and his siblings. But it was all necessary growing up where he had been reared.

I learned that his name was Jerry. Now as I was growing up, my friends and I would play a game about names, and it was a fact that most did not want to marry a George, Albert, Jerry, Fred, Melvin, or a Henry. Now that I am older I know that it is not about the name, but what is in the man.

Be proud to be linked to his name, because nowadays, if a Melvin, Henry, or Jerry can love you the way that God intended for you to be loved, then the name is unimportant.

I did think that Jerry had some issues though. For eight months, he was a perfect gentleman, who did not try anything with me. I thought that *something was either wrong with him,* or he was not that interested in me. So I got a little bored with him.

I did not realize at the time that a man or woman does not always have to show their love with their bodies, and that is what Jerry was trying to show to me. What he wanted me to know is that people can show their love and desire by their actions as well. He made me feel so comfortable around him. He would put me to sleep massaging my neck and back, when he would come to visit. Then he would talk to Ree about me and, *of course*, I always got the news from her later.

I think that Jerry secretly knew that she was telling me everything. It seemed to be all of what he could not say to me *face-to-face* himself, because he knew that I still had not given up all of my *wild ways*.

Even though I really liked him, I felt that *I had needs as well* that needed satisfying, and he was not offering that at the time. This was a *big hang up* and an *even bigger* mistake for me, because I still did not fully realize what I had right in front of me.

Jerry was that *diamond in the rough* that I kept searching for in the streets. What I was still out there looking for was waiting right next door to me, and I did not even realize it. Jerry was a *real* man. He was a *God-sent man*, and a very patient man as well. He was unlike the *boys* that I was still *hanging out* with in the streets.

There were times that he would see me outside of my house waiting for one of my numerous male friends. He would ask if I wanted to see some movies at his house, and I would reply that I was already waiting on someone to pick me up. He would then reply, "Well if not, just let me know. I'm here."

One time I had waited for my *guy friend* to come by and he did not show up. Jerry had already asked if I had wanted to come over. I gave him the same reply, *and in turn* he gave me the same reply.

Then about an hour or so later, he came out again *smiling*, asking had I changed my mind. I replied angrily, "No, I have not!"

Needless to say, I was *stood up* that night, and Jerry had wanted me to spend some quality time with him, but I would not. I was angry because I had been stood up, and because Jerry seemed both *relieved* and *content* that I was still out there, and not with some other man. I had just wasted my time in expectation of *Mr. Wrong*, when *Mr. Right* had been waiting tirelessly by the sidelines.

The race is definitely not given to the swift, or to the strong, but to the one who *endures* to the end, and Jerry was the winner that night. He knew it, but I did not.

However the Holy Spirit had been talking to me that evening, and that was *one of the few times* that I had been paying attention. Thank God that it was not another *missed* opportunity to have a decent man in my life, like some of the other guys that truly liked me, and I had just breezed past them.

Again that was the difference between what God had for me, and what I had for myself. So that is why Jerry remained on the scene. Which one will stand the *true test* of time, God's choice or yours? I have since discovered the answer to that question. God's plan will always *supercede* what you set out for yourself. *It is just that simple.*

As time went on I finally committed more to Jerry, but it still was not completely. My God knew exactly what I needed and He designed him *perfectly well*. He also knew that I was *still being me*, but He was already working on *me* too.

Even though I really cared for Jerry, he was just sort of *boring* to me at the time. Now I do believe in God's good and perfect will, and Jerry was and is God's special blessing for me. Trust, there were plenty of times that he should not have stayed with me, but he did anyway.

Finally we *became a couple* and moved in together. Even though we had been *shacking-up*, we realized that our *true blessings* would not come *until* we were pleasing God, and this was *definitely* not the way to do it.

In the meantime, I became pregnant and a baby boy was born. We also had begun to raise my little sister CoCo as well. At this point, we knew that we had to make things right before God because we had *a family* now.

Then we got married and it was the most *amazing* thing ever. *I can still remember.* Jerry and I could not stop laughing and smiling at one another after the ceremony. It was better than the first time that we met because we were *finally* pleasing God.

Neither one of us had *ever* experienced such bliss before, except for when our first baby, Javier, was born into the world.

It was awesome to finally be married to *Mr. Right*! God designed all of this in His own style…*GOD STYLE*!

CHAPTER 28

After the marriage, *one child became two*. However, with the second pregnancy things were very different. I did not want to listen to the doctor's recommendations for anything.

My second baby boy was born at one pound ten ounces, at twenty-six week's gestation, when a normal baby is born at forty weeks. The doctors had already warned me that I was very high risk when they discharged me from the hospital after a weeklong stay.

I had been discharged with the assurance that I would be on strict bed rest, and I could do nothing other than go to the bathroom and back. The doctor had warned, "You are very high risk, but we are going to take a chance and let you out today."

I had completed a series of optional steroid shots to the butt to enhance my baby's lungs, so the doctor felt that either way, it was now okay to go home. They had done everything that they could do to possibly ensure that the baby could survive *outside of me* at this point. Of course, still being very stubborn and hardheaded, I retreated home and started to clean the house. All that day I carefully completed all of the chores, much to the opposition of Jerry continuously fussing. "Poo you know that you need to do what you promised the doctor you would do! You need to sit down and stop cleaning up! What about this baby? Let's give *him* a chance!"

"Oh, Jerry, don't worry! Everything is fine! Stop fussing! I will be through soon, and then I will lay down!"

"Whatever. Just hurry up before I sit you down myself," Jerry nervously continued.

I did not feel anything then to hinder my duties. But hours later, at three in the morning, I knew that something was going terribly askew. "Jerry, wake up! I feel like I am going into labor!"

"Oh no, Poo! See I told you not to be up doing all of that stuff!"

"Please Jerry, I don't want to hear that right now! Just get me to the hospital please! I am starting to have contractions, and they are coming rather hard!"

When I got to the hospital, the same overnight staff was present again. Everyone was scolding me, yet trying to calm me down.

Present in the delivery room were several neonatal intensive care nurses and the gynecologist. One of the nurses came up to me and said, "Don't worry, we have our team waiting on him to arrive. He's going to be really tiny and will be fighting for his life. That is why we cannot medicate you, because he needs to be as alert as possible."

I did not care what pain I endured as long as my child was born and could survive. I carried the burden of my stupidity that had brought us there. I could only think that I was the reason for my baby's impending struggle.

What the hell had I been thinking? I was not superwoman! Now my newborn would come out bearing the brunt of my idiocy.

I started to cry with each extreme contraction, but I was not weeping for me. I was only hurt for what was happening to my tiny baby inside.

As the baby was born, I listened for a cry. Only silence gripped the air, as I screamed out to the team. "Is my baby okay?"

But nobody said anything.

"Is my baby okay?" Again there was stillness, as I looked over at Jerry. He was pale as a sheet as I continued to query him. "Jerry, please tell me, is my baby alright?" Yet he remained soundless.

CHAPTER 29

After delivering the afterbirth, I was rolled past the minute incubator, which held my baby. The only indication that he was alive, I viewed with my own eyes. One tiny little leg was raised up in the air. This miniature limb was wiggling vigorously all around.

As the team surrounded the baby, working diligently to stabilize him, I observed that he had been born severely premature. From the time that he was born, it took the doctor's about eight hours to come and tell me that he was still alive. I kept calling down to the nursery, but no one would give me any answers or details.

When the doctor walked into my room, I promptly asked him, "Doctor, is my baby still alive?"

"Yes, right now he is."

"Is he going to survive?"

"I cannot say right now, but there is only about a fifty-fifty chance for his survival."

With this information, the doctor departed as quickly as he had come in.

Right then my head seemed to want to explode. I could not call Rose because she was now *strung out* on crack.

Mommie and Poppie understood, but they really did not.

Butch could not help me either, because of what he also knew. My own sister Charlen had died from being born premature, plus he was still *dibbling and dabbling* with cocaine himself.

I wanted to call my cousin Dominique to vent, but I did not. Then I thought about calling my mother-in-law in Chicago. First I had to give her the news of the baby's sudden arrival. Then I had to explain to her the odds of his survival.

My *streetwise* sister-in-law Dee just happened to be there and asked, "Does he have a heart and a brain?"

"Yes, he does. He's just very small."

"Okay, well he'll live!" she exclaimed.

Even though what Dee asked me did not make any sense at the time, because it took more than just that for this baby to make it through, I still somehow believed what she said to be true. No sooner than I got off with my mother-in-law, Dominique was already calling. "Hey, girl, how are you doing? And how is the baby?"

"Dominique, I don't know. I only know that I messed up. I can't believe that this baby's life is hanging in the balance like this."

"Everything is alright. You just have to keep that word, and just pray that God will say the same. So in the meantime what are you going to name him?"

"I don't know yet. I want something with Jerry in it, because I am not having any more after this. Yet I still want it to symbolize God also. Because *He is the only hope* that we have now."

"How about this…? How about that…?" We continued to brainstorm. By the time that we had finished, his name had been chosen.

From that point on the baby's life hung in limbo. This was the longest three months and fifteen days that I have ever had to endure. But this little *preemie man* proved that he was up for the challenge.

He was given back to God in the choosing of his name, and *Christian* became *my little miracle child*. He has been very special to me ever since.

No sooner than Christian was born, I became pregnant once again. This time I planned it though, because I was still not sure that he would make it. In my young mind, I wanted to *make up for him*. After all, it had been my fault that he was born so early, and there was nothing that I could do about it now. Thereby, foolishly I figured that I could *replace him*, if the inevitable was to happen.

Christian's birth had also driven a wedge between Jerry and I that was not good for this young family that we had created.

During this time, I had no one close to call upon. Jerry did not understand my frustration because he secretly blamed me. Ree was away in college, and CoCo was still too young to comprehend. I did have Muddie, Mommie, Poppie, and Jerry's family. But for the most part I just wanted to be left alone.

When I needed them most, Rose and Butch were *caught up* in their drug usage, and cocaine did not allow them to feel much else. *They only cared about where they could get their next hit.* I could not even trust Rose to come into my house without stealing, and Butch was not too much better either.

These were the early nineties when *crack* had first come to light. This was a time of gang fights, drive-by shootings, and death in my small town. Almost weekly there was news of friends and acquaintances lost to the grips of drugs and violence.

Ree had gotten smart, though, and gone off to college. She esteemed to make life better for herself, so she got out of *the crack house*.

Then Dominique had gotten ill, so, virtually, this was the time that I began to grow up really fast.

Everything around town, and within my own life, was bad news then. *Now I know* as turmoil comes into your life you have to go to *the only One* who can offer a solution. He can help in any situation, any problem, or any circumstance, and that is God Almighty. *All you have to do is call upon His name.*

CHAPTER 30

Soon Jerry got tired of the way that our finances were going with all of the struggles and low paying jobs, and enrolled in school.

I was also working a low wage job, but was totally uninterested in going back to college at this time. I cannot tell you *what* I was thinking, because I had always craved knowledge before. I guess I had just begun to give up.

After my third child, another son, Justin, I started to think differently about life. I realized that I did not want to be on WIC and food stamps all of my life. We had gone through the first couple of children without public assistance, just by working hard. Jerry and I both had already experienced that *kind of life* growing up and had wanted something *very different* for *our family*. However, now it was becoming more and more overwhelming.

It was apparent that we had *too many kids too quickly*, and not enough resources *or education* to care for them adequately. *But it was not their fault!* So what do you do at that point? You do not just abandon them, you *get up* and *empower yourself* to do better, and *change your circumstances*.

Jerry had allowed me to stop working after Justin to keep down daycare costs, but I soon realized that he could not do it all by himself. I think that is when he became *baldheaded*. At least that is what my mother-in-law always said.

For a long while we struggled to make ends meet. We had three babies, *all* still in pampers, and a six-year old *little* sister, who had become very resentful that we were raising her instead of her parents, to add to the chaos.

My parents were still out getting high and doing their own thing, and by now our small wood-framed home had also become too small to accommodate us all.

Plus, we had no air conditioning in the middle of a *long* Texas summer. At this time, the kids were happy to ride in the car with air conditioning, and would cry when we turned down our street to go home.

Soon I began to seek employment anywhere to overcome our financial difficulties. We knew by now that it was definitely time to move into a better place, complete with air.

A few weeks later, I found a job at a fast food restaurant about fifteen miles away. I was *so* happy about it and just happened to be *in a place* that day where I could use the payphone without it being long distance. So I called Ree, who was *still* in college, despite now having her own baby; I wanted to tell her the good news.

She was *so* excited for me *at first*. Then she hesitated and asked, "Wait a minute, is this a fast food job?" At this point she made me feel too embarrassed to even reply, because she was right.

Somehow she already knew the answer and replied, "Since you are already so close to the airport, why don't you just go to look for a job there? Shaylyn is working at one of the bookstores and she said that they were hiring," referring to her best friend and former college dorm mate.

I did not feel like driving any further that day, however Ree made me feel so bad that I went to the airport. When I got there I started to ask different people for applications. I stopped by bookstores, various airline counters, and restaurants. Some people treated me nicely, and others were rather rude.

I still felt like *a nobody* too, so rejection really did hurt, and it almost made me give up that day and leave.

However, my last stop was at an airline counter where the employees treated me *so warm* and *so friendly*.

They even asked if I wanted to fill out the application there and I am glad that I did, because the way that I was feeling I would not have *ever* returned to turn that application back in. After all, I thought *who would want a GED test graduate to work for them?* My life's pathway had once again returned to haunt me.

CHAPTER 31

I did not feel worthy of anything but food service, but *I thank God for the angels* that He set forth in front of me in those employees. They told me what positions to apply for and everything. I must have really worn my discouragement on my face that day because they really seemed to care.

Since then I have learned that it is *always* good to follow the blessed pathway that God lays before you. You will always know when it is right because it just feels right, and there is *no hesitation*.

Sometimes you will even act before you think. That is when the Holy Spirit has taken over to tell you *what* to say, *when* to say it, and *how* to say it, and it is *always* perfect timing.

Obedience *is* a blessing, and staying that day to fill out the application became one of *the best* decisions of my life; and I know that it was *the Holy Spirit* working through my sister that led me to *the place* that has been *my livelihood* ever since.

From that day forward this airline kept calling me for different things to let me know that they were interested. I had two interviews, submitted a copy of my GED, and affidavits of unemployment, oh, and my drug test.

Even after the first interview, I felt that I had the job. It was just something that I could feel inside. Everything seemed to be *vibing* just perfectly. The interviewer was even massaging my back and telling me to calm down. She had to have been sent *straight from God*.

After all of this good news, we learned that I was pregnant *yet again*. This would now be our fourth child, and we knew then that we had to find a larger place. I also thought that this would be a *grand* time to get away from our small town living, partially because I was just embarrassed at being pregnant once more. But I was not shameful enough to stop doing what it took to get that way.

At first Jerry was rather reluctant to move. He had come from Chicago, and did not want the *big city* life anymore. But he knew that we needed better circumstances for our children and our own sanity, especially before a new child came into the world. So we finally came to the conclusion to move away.

We had *really* been struggling and my new pregnancy only added to the worries; however we realized that it had ultimately been our *slip up* yet again, and we would not be looking at any other alternatives but to have another happy healthy baby despite our financial hardships. This was our choice, and we would be *the only ones* to decide *how* or *what* our lives would be like, and how many kids we would eventually have.

It was not the best time, especially now that I possibly had the chance at a real good job. *But is there ever a best time, when a pregnancy is unplanned?*

During this period of time that I was waiting to be hired, Jerry and I made the conscious decision to *step out on faith*, and move about thirty miles away, to Houston.

Even though the *move-in special* only lasted for three months and we knew from there we could not afford our place without better jobs, we still took the chance.

Since Jerry's job was still thirty miles back home, he continued to drive back and forth, still praying for better. He was farther away, but I was now only ten minutes away from my desired job at the airlines; except I still did not know *when*, or *even if*, they would call me for training.

Our move took place in July, and by mid-August Jerry was then called with a much better job offer. His schooling had helped him along and he now had two solid job offers, making much more than he currently was, and we were ecstatic. He decided on the one closest to us, despite the pay being about a thousand dollars less per year in salary; however, it wasn't much to lose for a closer location.

Seven months into my pregnancy, in September, I also got called for the new hire training class with the airlines. This had been the call that I had been waiting for all along. God had finally answered each and every prayer for us. Stepping out on faith proved to be a real blessing, and we were just about to *reap the benefits* of it.

Suddenly my joy turned into worry because I wanted this job so badly; but now that I was pregnant, I did not know if they would hire me knowing my circumstances. Thereby, I decided to take the chance and not tell anyone. Once I completed training and was officially hired, then they would not be able to let me go.

My plan to keep quiet went well for about two weeks into training. I stayed to myself and did not try mingling in the various circles of new hires. I was there and did not want anyone to talk to me. Then by the third week of training one of the girls, Theresa, asked me a question. Her comment was "Now you can tell me if this is offensive or not, but are you pregnant, or are you just *funny built?*"

I was both shocked and offended, however she was almost a foot taller than I was; and I did not want to have to fight or take the chance at losing the position that I had worked so hard to get, because I was still *quite the hothead.*

My response was rather cool, but I admitted that I was pregnant and I told her that I did not want anyone to know it. Why did that become the topic of the next class? Because not only was the trainer herself pregnant, but another girl in our new hire class was as well; I never realized it though, so then I knew that I was okay.

Then surprisingly, on the last day of class with a final facing me, I went into labor. Everyone was telling me to go home, but I was determined to finish that exam. After all I had not come that far to give up now. Had I not completed the test, I would have not been able to complete the training class, and I would not have been hired. That day, in active labor, I made a *100* on the test and completed training with the second to the highest average in the class. Remember, I was never a dummy, but just a person that had made some real dumb decisions in the past.

Right after the exam I went to the hospital, and later we delivered our fourth child.

CHAPTER 32

Jerry was always present in the delivery room *and* he *always* did the most work with each new baby. I was always *the lazy one*, despite me being the pregnant one. Our fourth baby, Jessica, became our only little girl, and we were so pleased. After having three boys, it was like we were starting all over again.

We had to buy a lot of new pink clothes, although, she still wore a lot of blue *hand-me-downs* over the years as well.

Later that next year, I was diagnosed with tumors that caused me to have a hysterectomy at age twenty-four. I can still recall Ree coming in during my recovery, while I was *still* in lots of pain. "Poo, Poo are you okay?"

"Oooh, I am in pain! Oooh, I am hurting!"

"Poo, are you okay?" Ree kept asking. She was trying to talk to me and I was moaning deliriously in and out of consciousness. I could see her and I was trying to talk to her, but my mouth would not move.

What we laugh about today is, even though we do not always get along, I truly know that she *always* has my back. That is the way that sisters *should* be.

I can recall that during my various stages of consciousness, Ree just sat there sobbing, because I was in so much distress and could not respond to her questions. Now I tease her about it because it really was funny after the fact, but not while I was wailing in pain.

It is always great to laugh. As they say, *"Laughter keeps the heart merry, and is like a medicine to the soul."*

I can also remember a nun coming into this Catholic hospital room to counsel with me afterwards, and she just did not know what to say. At the time I did not understand her hesitation until she said, "I am so sorry for you, but there is always adoption."

Then I looked at her and replied, "Adoption? I already have four kids, *and* a little sister that I am raising! So I have five children at home!"

The awkwardness apparently leaving as the nun said excitedly, "Five kids! Well then *you are* already blessed!" All I could do is smile through all of the tedious pain and stitches, because she was definitely right about that.

"Five little ones at home!" I began to think. Then I started to understand why God had blessed me with all of these babies back to back.

He already knows what each person needs, and He truly knew *what* I needed, and *when* I needed it!

HE IS SO AWESOME!

CHAPTER 33

Life was starting to become good to us, however it was still somewhat stressful. Jerry and I were making money and blowing just as much as we could make. Even though he was more conservative and tried to save as much as he could, I was constantly doing just the opposite; and most of the time he allowed me to do whatever I wanted to do.

Everybody always commented on just how good of a husband I had, and Jerry truly *was* indeed.

Even though, we were both working late hours and hardly seeing each other, we still managed to hang in there. We were so in love at this point that we were just having a good time being in each other's company anytime that we could. We enjoyed our family time together too.

Then I met a homeless man named Bill, rummaging through our apartment dumpsters, and befriended him. Even though I did not like Bill's lifestyle, I constantly witnessed to him about God and blessed him every time I saw him. He would always tell me, "God has given you to me as my guardian angel, and I love you *and* Him for that!"

I would *then* always reply back, "I love you too, Bill." I tried relentlessly to bring happiness to him, and he truly brought happiness to me also. I loved to see Bill smile and to know that maybe one day my small contributions to his life would somehow enable him to think and do better as well.

I even offered him an airplane ticket back to Ohio. He had come from there and, if it would offer him a better lifestyle, I reluctantly wanted him to go.

We had to have been the oddest-looking couple around, *whenever and wherever* we were together; a younger middle-class-looking black girl, and an older-looking vagrant Caucasian man. But we were the best of friends, no matter what. I truly did love Bill and he loved me as well.

Butch and Rose also seemed to both be *somewhat* off of drugs and rotated in keeping all of the kids. As their child, I loved the time that we all spent together. We had so much fun all together.

Butch would tell Rose, "Ooh, girl, you're looking good again. Come on in the room with me." Then he would play like he was chasing her, while she would just laughingly say, "Butch, leave me alone!"

Those were some really happy times, aside from the good times that we had experienced as a family when Ree and I were children.

Rose had someone new in her life, Allen, and Butch was just going it solo and enjoying hanging out with the grandkids and us. He and Jerry were taking lots of trips to Chicago. Then my coworker Theresa and I were becoming the best of friends as well.

Everything was just copasetic. Just like the calm before the storm, it was all going so well.

And then…

CHAPTER 34

One night, while at work, I called Rose to check on the kids. This was Theresa's and my daily ritual before eating lunch. We both had to check on our kids first. It was always *the norm* for us, but this time would not be so normal after all.

I will never forget Rose's words on the other end of the line when she said, "Poo, Dominique died tonight."

"What?" I could not have heard her right. "What did you say, Rose?"

"Dominique died tonight."

"No, Rose! No!" Her words cut me like a knife. "No!" I began to fall down as my legs became weak. This just could not be happening! It just could not be! Dominique was just too young to die. I began to cry out.

In the past, I always seemed to have the answers to everything. I knew what it took to survive and I prided myself on always being in control. But this time it just was not happening.

Losing my cousin was one of the hardest things for me to endure. When she closed her eyes, a part of me died with her.

In the days following, reality started to quickly elude me. As I bore the hurt and guilt, only my faith in God could come back full circle to pull me through.

We had never talked about Dominique's illness, but everyone already knew. We always said that we loved each other at the end of each phone call, but some things were just left *unsaid*. I had been so busy lately that I had not been calling her as often as I should have been, but she already understood that I would talk to her when I could.

After all she was my favorite cousin and she had hung in with me through all of the various phases of my life. She had been the only one there for my abortion when we were sixteen.

"Why her?" I continued to ask myself. "I had been so promiscuous in my teenage years. Yet I was still living? Why had God allowed me to live? I should have been preparing for the grave instead of Dominique," so I thought.

During the week before her funeral, we all seemed to be living in a complete state of denial. This just could not be happening. Even though the reality was there, I just did not seem to grasp it.

The day of the funeral Ree, Jerry, Rose, Aunt Brea, and I were busy trying to get dressed, and still attempting to get to the church on time.

Even though it was still a sad occasion, we tried to maintain by cracking a few jokes along the way. We were all just trying to keep our spirits up, as the music played softly in the background. To this day, Ree and I can still recall the very song that was playing on the radio as Jerry turned the corner to the church.

The big white hearse parked in front of the church welcomed our view. This became the realization to what was actually taking place on the inside.

All of a sudden, it began to hurt all over again. As the tears flowed, we entered the sanctuary. Up that long pathway to the casket, to see Dominique lying in state.

"No, not her! Why her?" I continued to silently question. My grief was unimaginable!

"Why can't you just get up, Dominique? Please get up!" I continued to search for answers. Barely teasing her twenties, Dominique was too young to leave this earth.

She had just actually begun to know what life was really about, and now she was dead. She was so beautiful, so poised, and so smart, but her potential would never be realized now. For it had all come to an abrupt end with the closing of her eyes.

All during the service I wept, *we wept*, all of my cousins wept. We all continued to embrace each other in an attempt to console one another, but there was no solace in what we all had to endure.

This was definitely one of *the* saddest funerals that I have ever had to attend.

We were all around the same age, in our late teens to early twenties, so it was all quite hard to understand. Words could never express Dominique's loss, but I guess that is the case with any loved one that passes on.

As the funeral came to a dismal end, the pallbearers paced quietly past carrying Dominique's coffin. At that moment, I extended my hand out to touch the casket for the very last time. As I laid my palm down on its flat surface I felt weak once more, and my tears began to flow once again. This last contact became *my own special way* to say farewell to my favorite cousin, confidant, and cohort.

For an instant I was rendered speechless and somewhat overcome by the entire moment. I began to feel the chilled firmness of this pale pink casket, as it seemed somewhat symbolic of the sheer essence of nonexistence, which is what I was so foolishly seeking.

Dominique had taken so many wonderful times, secrets, and shared memories, with her to the grave. I just could not take it. This day became the commencement of my dismay, and that night I contemplated suicide. I could no longer endure the pain of continuing to live on, while Dominique had become just a memory. Even though I had a budding family at home, I could not see past the loss or the visions of that pastel coffin; for I bore the guilt of being amongst the living, as Dominique was now unexpectedly departed.

She was so attractive and suddenly I was so hideous that I felt that I no longer deserved to live. This was a very outlandish thought, but I took it rather seriously. Crazily I felt that I needed to take care of the problem that I thought to be myself. So soon quite meticulous thoughts began to creep up into my head, as I set out to *personally* do something about it.

CHAPTER 35

As I gazed at Jerry's .45-caliber pistol, I began to draw it near. It was so heavy, but it seemed to be just what I needed. After all, I had a .25-caliber, but it seemed to lack the power of the larger weapon, which is what I felt that I desired to complete the task. For an instant I went into a daze as if the devil was subtly nudging me and taking me right into a *suicidal zone*.

The sounds of my children's laughter filled the distance, as Jerry played with them in the front room. They would never know what had actually transpired in the bedroom that day. For all I needed was a release from the excruciating pain. How selfish of me. My grasp on reality was temporarily lacking.

As I pulled the gun closer to my head, the notion of God quickly interrupted my absence of thought. For a moment I began to think as I swiftly dropped the gun. I could no longer go through with it after all.

Then God's everlasting strength within made me pick up a pen instead. I had no willpower at that moment, but what was inside subtly moved me into another kind of action. Even as a child I had always been acknowledged for carrying a book around with me, and equally so, I was a writer in my own rite. However, writing came more natural when I was distraught, and along with the anger and the pain, this seemed just the right combination to purge everything from inside onto the pages of my journal.

I wrote Dominique a letter to *bid her adieu*, and it was one of the hardest things that I have ever had to do. The finality of it was agonizing.

But to the present, I have kept this memoir for my own personal inspiration and motivation. Dominique would have wanted it that way.

For a while I also sought medical treatment and was prescribed an antidepressant. I took the medicine for a while but I hated the side affects. So one day I came to a sound conclusion that God was my *only* doctor, and my faith *could* and *would* bring me through this. That day I threw away a nearly full, prescription bottle of pills, and from that day forth, I began to rely on God once again for my strength and encouragement.

The assurance in God became my sole closure, and I realized that He *alone* was my *only* source.

In retrospect, it is clear that the devil desires each of us and he almost had me that depressing April night. But God was still in control and my consolation came in Him, not in a pistol trigger, bullet, or drugs. Only *He* has the real authority to guide you through. Please believe that.

If someone contemplates suicide, realize that thoughts come naturally; however, it is our choice to proceed with them or not. Please do not be foolish. Suicide does not pacify the hurt; it only inflicts more of it.

Things can change with the blinking of an eye. Just as God can *show up* and *show out* for you *and* your circumstances. No love, no person, no situation is worth your happiness.

Dominique would have told me the same thing had I been in her presence with the same fatal thoughts. That was just the type of individual that she was, and for that I truthfully adore and miss her deeply.

TO YOU MY BEAUTIFUL COUSIN

CHAPTER 36

As our life together continued, Jerry and I sustained many trials and tribulations along the way. Mainly financial, but I still had a strong spirit of *whoredom* within me as well.

Even though I had a great man at home, I still found comfort along the way in new relationships and a few former boyfriends alike, who never seemed to be that far away.

Whenever there were conflict or disputes between us, I sought out the affection of the other men. Instead of attempting to find solutions, I did nothing to help our situation. It appeared that we now had more chaos in our lives than ever before.

The kids were growing up. Jerry was continuing to work hard and raise them, for the most part alone. Despite what was happening at home, he never let it affect his job performance, or let it prevent him from being *mom and dad* to the children.

All I was becoming was the extra finances needed to operate the household. I was rapidly becoming *nonexistent* in my family's lives. I was really losing myself in the midst.

After a while, things really began to go downhill to the point of us both discussing divorce.

I still did not see the error of my ways, so I continued to do what I wanted to do. I had blinders on and I did not want to change at that time.

Butch, who had been the same way with Rose, would sometimes just shake his head in utter disgust. When I would return home from one of my many rendezvous' he would say, "Girl, I just don't understand why you are doing this. You need to keep your butt at home where you belong! What's gotten into you?"

My reply would always be, "How can you talk? *Remember I am just like you.*"

And he would reply, "And I was stupid back then too!" Butch knew just what I was doing, because he had been that same person not too many years prior. Knowing just what kind of treacherous pathway I was taking, Butch tried relentlessly to intervene. He attempted to talk to me repeatedly, but my ears were not hearing. He would say, "What is wrong with you girl? Didn't you learn anything from me?"

I kept trying to do better, but temptation was too immense, and most of the time it succeeded. I truly valued these other men, and enjoyed the pleasures of my sin. Even though I realized later that there was no love there, only lust.

This was the devil's ploy to steal, kill, and destroy my family, and he almost had me too. We always seem to blame the devil for what we go through in life, but sometimes it is our own flesh that wants to do wrong.

Remember we are all dirt, however beautiful and great looking, still nothing but dirt housed in skin. We are all like filthy rags; sinners who have all fallen short of God's glory. Now do we lie down and succumb? Or do we continue to fight to be on the pathway of righteousness?

Are we seeking God along life's journey? Or are we taking the wide pathway of destruction yet again, and again, and again? The decision is yours, *and yours alone…*

CHAPTER 37

After a few years, we moved back to the little country town that we had happily left behind. We were blessed with my aunt's home, with no rent to pay, and we hopped on it.

"What better way to try to get back on top?" we had thought. This would be our chance to save some money and also to get back to quiet living, and at first it was great. Through it all I had never stopped talking to my friend Bill, the homeless guy, so I had to make sure to let him know that we were moving away from Houston.

Before we moved Bill gave me a plastic ring that he had made and I wore it proudly next to my ring finger, because I always jokingly said that he was my *second husband*.

After each time, I looked down at that simple plastic ring; I would take a moment to pray for him. Bill had to be okay, and since I was not around him, I knew that God was going to take care of him for me.

I wore that ring for years until one day it just popped off of my finger; and, at that moment, my heart suddenly dropped because I then wondered what had happened to Bill.

I felt that either he had just died, or he no longer needed his self-designated guardian angel anymore. For a moment I thought about it, but I knew that there was no way for me to ever know, so I just prayed for him and let it go.

For a while afterward everything went rather smoothly. I even figured that coming home might have been a positive change for us, despite Butch's reluctance.

But soon *I* crept up once again…

I had returned to my family trying to be both a good wife and mother, but soon *I* became the same shameless demon that *I* had been attempting to suppress for quite some time. *I became that same lustful creature within* that was now trying to rear its ugly head once more.

I met up with an *ex-boyfriend* who seemed to still be very interested. How many people know that they always are when you are no longer available? But I decided against him, because he had once been an *associate* of Jerry's as well. Wow, talk about *your friends*! Do not ever say what *they will* and *will not* do, because *they* may just surprise you!

After the temptations of *Mr. Ex*, I attempted to *lighten up* in messing around again; however, as living got more peaceful, I once again became more forward in my escapades. That same spirited demon that I despised in Butch was slowing taking me away as well.

At this time, my eyes were always on the prowl. I was always looking for *yet another* person to spend time with, other than the family that I had been *blessed* with.

I soon found comfort in the arms of another man quite a bit older than me. Monty seemed to have everything going well for himself. He was definitely unlike all of the others that I had been *acquainted* with since I had returned to town.

He had a decent job and a few side hobbies to his credit, and he seemed to be very interested in me. At least that is what his eyes seemed to say each time that I saw him, and soon I acted upon that visual communication.

He would tell me, "I could take care of you if you leave your husband, and I don't do the kid thing either. Just leave them with him too."

With that, I told him, "Don't even worry about it. I am not leaving my husband or kids. But we can enjoy this time that we have together right now."

What kind of woman leaves her spouse, or better yet her *CHILDREN* for another man that she barely even knows? I was not about to do this. That had been a promise that I had made to myself when Rose left us. I would never leave my kids the way that she did us.

But I still chose to *gallivant* with *a jerk* for the moment, *who was not looking for anything* but a good time; although that is *all* that I was looking for as well. I was not thinking about leaving Jerry for anyone! *"Having your cake and eating it too"* was much too good for that!

CHAPTER 38

This relationship was fine for *a spell* until I realized that it was *never about me*. Monty just wanted to add another *notch* onto his belt. How could I have been so wrong about him? But we all know that *you will* reap what you have sown. Was I expecting him to treat me any better than I was treating Jerry at the time?

It still hurt me though to feel used. No one wants to feel that way! But *really* what was it that I was expecting out of a relationship that was cursed from the start anyway?

Another day I made plans to go out with someone else. Jerry had ironed my clothes for me and was *watching* the kids as well. He did not even ask me where I was going this night. *What kind of fool was I back then?*

As I sat outside of my house waiting on a phone call from the *other guy*, I began to *ponder* on a few things. Then before the devil could get a *good grip* on me, the Holy Spirit spoke to me *so clearly*. He reminded me of what I had just left behind, and what I was *yet* waiting on.

It was as if I was replaying and visualizing all of the scenes back in my head at that moment. The Holy Spirit showed me Jerry inside working tirelessly, taking care of *our* kids, cooking, and cleaning as well.

Then I pictured him sending me off without even an utterance of disagreement for leaving him behind. "Just be careful, Poo," he said.

Then I *reminisced* on just how happy we had once been. It had been *years* since we had truly been one. Nonetheless, I knew that what I was seeking *in the streets* was not what I needed.

But when you are *caught up* in a certain kind of lifestyle, it is *extremely difficult* for the blinders to fall off. It is so hard to see past what you are doing, which is the *façade* that the devil has set up for you. This is *the trap* that certainly turns to damnation, if you allow it to, but I just thank God that *He* still had His hand on me.

I will not say that it has not been an *uphill battle* though, but I knew that what God blessed, which was Jerry's and my marriage, was the only option for me to choose.

At that point, I got out of my car and went back into the house, and from that day forth I became his wife *again*. Even though we had been through *so much*, the prayer that was spoken over our marriage was *still* working in the spiritual realm for us.

Even though *I* had stepped out of the marriage *we* had successfully *kept it in the bonds of holy matrimony*, thanks be to God and Jerry's *God-given* patience for me. By right, he should have been gone *a long time ago*. I was not that special, but I guess God thought otherwise, *even in my sin*.

That was just *the twins,* grace and mercy working overtime in and *for my life*, and I really needed *them* too! *Thanks be to God for His everlasting love for me!*

CHAPTER 39

The day that the phone rang and the person on the other end asked for Butch, I already knew in my heart what was really going on. The *Holy Spirit* had never left me in the dark on anything and this time was *no different*.

As I attempted to put it *to the back of my mind*, I was already a *million miles away* in my head. In the distance, I could hear my dad answering every question from the caller, but what stuck in my head is when he said, "Okay, I can be there tomorrow."

I suddenly felt *sick to my stomach* because I already knew that *life was suddenly about to throw another curve ball* within our lives, and this time we were not going to be as *resilient* to bounce right back.

You know, *along life's journey* everyone encounters *challenges*, however there is that one *life-changing* event that puts your life in *total perspective*, but I never expected this to happen. Not in a million years could this be *suddenly* happening to me, *or to us*.

We had already been through so much, but this was *truly* one of the hardest things that I had ever encountered, and life *truly* would not ever be the same because of it.

The next day Butch found out that he had lung cancer, and to him it was an *instant death sentence* because this same awful disease had taken Papa Bill so many years earlier also.

He had seen the pain, the agony, and already knew what the outcome *most likely* would be, but Butch's own premonitions had already prepared him for this anyway.

After all, he had *just* lost his oldest brother, Uncle Jr., to cancer just six months prior to his own diagnosis, and Butch had come away from that experience expressing that *he would be next*, and that he would never live to be fifty.

I kept telling him *not to speak that way* but he would not stop saying it, and sadly, Butch's words became truth only six months after this phone call at the age of *forty-nine*. He already knew it, and felt that he had been living on *borrowed time* anyway.

However, this day became *his reality* and he knew what needed to be done, but still made one last attempt to turn the other way. Butch had never *really* stopped completely drugging, drinking, and messing around. As he had gotten older, he had only *slowed down*. But what was in him was never *too far* behind.

Even though he expected *me* to be something other than what he was, my thoughts had always been that the *apple never fell far from the tree*, which was not scripture, but *my own* personal philosophy.

So I lived my life by that excuse to justify everything that I did wrong. That seemed to make it all right, so I thought. I looked nothing like him; nevertheless, inside I was *all* him.

It was very funny how Butch was one of five brothers and two sisters, and the boys *all* mostly had daughters, who were like their fathers before them. I was no different from my cousins, or from this *curse* that had loomed and lingered over us all. This *spirit of whoredom* was deeply embedded within us. Some just displayed it more openly than the others, and I was one of those that let it shine brightly like a neon street sign.

In the doctor's office had been one of my uncles Ryan, Aunt Brea, Butch, and me.

The doctor seemed to *beat around the bush* nervously for a moment with a bunch of small talk, until my dad redirected him and reminded him that he had been summoned there for a consult.

The doctor then proceeded forth as his words jabbed like a knife *deep* in the side. "From the results of your x-rays, we believe that you have lung cancer."

I could feel my heart suddenly stop for a moment, as my head dropped in utter disbelief. It was almost as if we had become *sus-*

pended in time for a moment. This just could not be happening to him, or to us, or to my family. No, this could not be true. However, it was quite real.

We had always survived whatever life had *thrown out*, but we all knew the results of a cancer diagnosis, especially lung cancer. At this point, no one was living in faith, but only dealing with the reality of this diagnosis, which again was not scripture.

We had already *fast-forwarded* to the end and felt that we knew the outcome of this. It was all so clear, but just for the moment *unspoken*. No matter how quiet we were, we all knew that this was totally devastating! This just could not be happening to us! What had we done to deserve this? This was always my question when something seemed to be wrong. But is it always because of something that we have done?

We have all fallen short of the glory, but it is *all in God's knowing*, as to *how* and *when* we leave this earth. We are all accountable for our circumstances and attribute, *for the most part*, to our own demise depending on how we live our lives.

I had to learn that over the years, because I was so analytical. I was always trying to figure things out. But just when you think you know, how many know that God comes at you from another angle?

The night of the *doctor's visit* became Butch's *enlightenment*. Everything that he had been doing in the past suddenly came to an *abrupt* halt.

He talked in great detail that afternoon about everything that had to be taken care of before he left. He wanted everything to be handled, from *the kids to the grandkids*. He needed this to be done soon and the way that he wanted it.

We assured him that everything would be okay, and that he must believe that all would be well.

By this time, I had already dealt with the news alone, and had already cried it out, and was now ready for *the fight*. Unlike any other battle, I was ready to tread into the *unknown* positively and faithfully. Yet the uncertainty was still quite scary.

But I knew that it was *best left in God's hands* at this point, because I could do nothing to stop it or to cure it myself. Even though, I was *out of my comfort zone*, I knew that only God possessed this kind of power and I had to rely *solely* on Him for an answer.

But Butch was not ready to hear this yet. Because of all that he had been dreaming about, he already knew that he was going to succumb and depression had already set in for *the kill*. I could see in his eyes what he was about to seek, and it *was not* God at this particular time. He was devastated, but he had to know that he could not do it alone. He needed help that no one else but God could give him.

As I cried, I attempted to stop him from leaving. I knew where he would find his comfort that night and I did not want to see that happen anymore.

He had to fight! He had to stop destroying himself over and over. But he was not yet ready for that.

As I pulled him back by the arm crying, he proceeded to leave out of the front door to get away from me. As he left, he said, "I've got to get out of here! I'll be back! I'm alright!"

As night came and went, I tossed, turned, and *PRAYED*. I already knew what was happening out in the streets with him, and all I could do is helplessly lean on God *yet* another time for strength and solace.

For one more night Butch indulged in his wrongdoing. Instead of leaning on God this night, he went out and got as high as he could get. He drank and drank as well, from one place to the next. But for every drug addict or alcoholic, from experience, they are usually trying to mask a deep hurt or an issue in their lives, or pasts that is not going to be resolved in the bottle, or in a pill, or powder.

Everyone is seeking happiness but running from *who, or what*, can truly make them happy, and often looking in the opposite direction for the help that they are lacking. That is why they are still in the midst of their problems and still not discovering what they really need.

Mind-altering substances *are not of God* but people often use them as a *coping mechanism*. Even though they are seeking, they are still not looking. Does that make sense? How wrong can they be?

That is why they *sober up* from their indulges with the same hurt as they had before, sometimes with *more* on their plates than they started with.

That night Butch did just that but there was just one catch; no matter how hard he tried, he failed at it. What he was trying to accomplish would not happen for him this time. For every drink, every hit that he took that night; it could not mask his pain.

Although Butch was running, God was right there, everywhere he turned. *"Thus far, and no further...."* He was not going to *get high* this night, because God was *now* talking directly to him. But it was up to him to listen. *But would he?*

CHAPTER 40

That morning Butch returned home, with a whole new outlook on life. He was *finally* ready to fight, so whatever happened now, he was ready to deal with it.

After smoking for about thirty-four years, he stopped *cold-turkey*. He gave his full pack of cigarettes to Jerry to dispose of them.

We discussed his night, and what we would do from this day forth.

You know, *everyone* is given a chance to live life the way that they want to. Everyone has choices, whether good or bad. They are theirs to make. But with every decision just know that there are consequences.

How do you approach it? What do you do? You shall reap a harvest, whether good or bad, for your choices. Believe it or not... *"the Word does not lie...."*

Butch knew that God was his *only* source, and only then did he begin to transition into the Christian that he knew would please his Father. Drugs became a part of the past and family time began to take precedence over everything.

He decided on surgery to remove his left lung, as an option to hopefully treat his disease. Prior to surgery though, there were a few things that he had to do just to ensure that he was strong enough for this procedure.

As we sat at each appointment, Ree and I would laugh with Butch and joke about everything.

We were both in college at the time. She was in nursing school, and my major was political science, which was *my passion*. But somehow we still found time to make each and every doctor's appointment anyway. We all needed this time together, and Butch needed his daughters' support as well, since Rose was still smoking crack then and did not have another care in the world.

The last appointment before the procedure, I likened to a *cattle call*. Every person scheduled for surgery was summoned to go to a common area, up a hallway, and around in another department. As we all followed behind this one individual taking us to the next area, *it was so quiet*.

I could feel the spirits of everyone as we walked. I could feel the tenseness, the anxiety, and the pain. I could feel the stress behind all of the smiles and solemn faces. It was like lambs being led to slaughter and I suddenly felt depression creeping upon me, but I began to pray to myself for each one of these persons and their families. *Thank God that I knew what to do.*

At that moment I felt the stress ease, at least from my spirit, so I believed God that everyone else's had subsided as well. Everyone in there needed a comfort, and God was the *ONLY* source that they had. So if He needed to use an *adherent*, that day I had to answer the call.

Once we got to where we needed to be I attempted to study, but it was as if the Holy Spirit was calling me to pray with this one couple.

I tried to ignore *the voice within me* but I just could not continue to sit still at that moment. I did not even know how receptive that they would be to me; nevertheless, I was obedient.

As I arose from my book, I asked if they needed prayer, and they replied, "Yes." This gentleman was having the same kind of surgery as Butch, the day before him.

As I began to pray with my hand touching his chest, I began to feel the Holy Spirit take over while I prayed for his anxiety, his uncertainty, his faith, and for his wife's strength. It was *as if* this is what they needed at the time, and the Holy Spirit just needed a willing body to *convey the message*. After I completed my prayer, we embraced.

When I returned to my seat between Butch and Ree, they were both very silent. Then I heard Butch say, "She just needed some attention, messing with those people." We then began to laugh hysterically. Butch really needed that amusement to help him through the moment, and it did break the silence that we all had between us too.

The day of surgery was a time of extreme anxiety. As I studied for a psychology test, I sat and I sat, waiting and praying.

My aunt, uncles, and sister went on chatting and laughing in the distance, as I continued to quietly think about what was taking place in that operating room. I was totally *oblivious* to what was going on around me.

Inwardly I began to reflect on how much I was *indeed* like my father, *even down to our names*, which were different by only one letter, from the first to the middle names.

I pondered on how our signatures were extremely similar, and on how I believed that we were so close in tune that we *even thought the same thoughts* at times.

We even had the same kind of emotions and we carried the same pain, struggling within ourselves. It was as if we were *twins* being separated from each other, and I briefly wondered if I would ever see him alive once again.

Butch and I had never been able to tell each other that we loved each other, even though we both already knew it. I had always seen the way he watched me, as though looking into a *mirrored image* of his own mind and soul. It was utterly amazing that we could be so different on the outside, *yet* so much alike on the inside. *What I loathed in the past is what I became proud of in the present.*

When Butch came out of surgery he was in a massive amount of agony, despite the large dosage of morphine that was being pumped through his intravenous tubing.

In the recovery room, it *tormented* me to see him suffering, but there was nothing that I could do to *carry his pain* for him. If I could have, I would have definitely *bore his torch* that day.

"Butch say it with me. The Lord is my Shepherd, I shall not want," Aunt Brea began to quote, as Butch simultaneously attempted to speak *Psalm: 23* as well.

"*The Lord is my Shepherd*, ooh it hurts!" He then stopped mid-sentence and began to wail out in pain. As I gazed into his face, his big beautiful eyes seemed to expose the *intense emotions* of what he was clearly experiencing. It was as if a substantial part of my heart was being *ripped away*, however I had to be strong through it all.

> *Lord, please in the name of Jesus, take this pain from my daddy. Please, Father! Please, Lord I ask that You would help Butch through this all, and thank You that this surgery has been victorious, in Jesus' mighty name we pray, Amen.*

After I prayed with Butch, I abruptly left the room. For this was all that my sanity could bear. In the hallway the doctor exclaimed, "The surgery was a success! We did end up taking the entire left lung, but he should recover fully." The doctor claimed that the surgery had been triumphant and from then on, Butch grew stronger and stronger each day.

When he was discharged from the hospital, he began to spend a lot of time with his close friends, trying to do the right thing. He was still quite a jokester, now just with an oxygen tank, to help him breathe. Although it was very funny to know that if a canister of air ran out in four hours while he was gone, you could bet that he was calling in three and a half hours to have his concentrator on once he got there. We would laugh about this all of the time.

Oxygen was *not* going to keep him from running the streets, even though it was now just in a more positive way than before. He really enjoyed life now and did not take it for granted; and he expressed to *everyone* about just how bad cigarettes were for them.

For a while things were really good. Then all of a sudden Butch started to have more problems breathing. One oxygen concentrator became two, and they were suddenly on the maximum level that they could go. He knew something else was going on then, and soon he could not get out like he used to.

He went in for more tests on his remaining lung and came home that day hardly able to breathe. He was soon hospitalized again in intensive care. This time the prognosis was *very bleak*.

CHAPTER 41

That day I had been home when the doctor called to give me the news. The doctors did not even know if he would make it out of the hospital this time. Butch was definitely in critical condition, and his life now *hung in the balance*.

I was summoned to the hospital immediately. I must have done *a hundred miles an hour* until I got there. The hospital ride was only about twenty to thirty minutes away, but it seemed like hours.

Once I got there, Butch was in the room alone. His eyes were filled with extreme fear and hopelessness. I could feel his disappointment. He had just been given the same news. His death had become more imminent than ever before.

He only had one lung and *would not* be a good candidate for a transplant because of the cancer. It had now spread into his right lung and it was *just a matter of time*. He was given the news that he was now terminal, with only about six months to live. The doctors could do no more for him. This was truly devastating to him as it was to all of us.

Ree had now come in and talked to Butch about how death was a part of life… *eternal life* that was. She explained to him that none of us remembered coming into the world. And, just as unknown as that was, death was feared only because of our fear of the unknown.

She also told him just how great it was for the death of one of *God's saints*. These words did work because they comforted him, but it still did not change the fact that he was now dying.

Before I left the hospital that night, I attempted to tell Butch that I loved him. Even as the words formed in my mouth, I could not speak them.

I tried again and again. "I…I love…uhh…" "I…I love…uhh," I repeated.

I couldn't do anything else but laugh, as Butch responded, "Yeah, yeah, Poo, I already know," with a big "blow off" wave and smirk. Instantly I felt sheer relief, because I realized that neither one of us could say the *L-O-V-E word* to each other.

We had gone through so much volatility when I was a teenager, and I had harbored so much resentment for him in the past that it had toughened each of our hearts to one another. He knew that I adored him and I knew it also. *So did we actually have to verbalize it?* We both proved it every day, even though it was really left unsaid.

As I was leaving the room the doctor came in to speak with Butch. "Have you decided where you will be staying at this point? You can always go to an assisted living center or…"

"He's coming home with me," I sharply interrupted.

"Oh, okay, well as long as he is still stable tomorrow, he will probably be discharged the day after."

"That's fine."

"But, Poo," Butch replied apprehensively. "Are you sure about this?"

"Haven't you already been staying with us anyway? Alright, don't ask anymore questions then!"

"Okay then, I am coming back home to die," Butch said with an unexpected relief.

"No, excuse me, that is one thing that I do not want to *ever* hear again, Butch! You are coming home to *LIVE*! Okay?"

"Whatever you say, Poo," he sarcastically retorted as I started to exit the room, continuously smiling at him as I proceeded to shut his hospital door.

Upon closing the door, my grin suddenly began to diminish as I started to deal with the *realism* that my father was indeed terminal and most likely would not live too much longer.

This depressing account was all too hard to endure, but I was still very much ready to assist Butch in his astringent battle until the conclusion. So we made the choice for him to come home *to die*.

CHAPTER 42

As his brothers packed him across the threshold of my front door, I spoke out that he was now entering into a place of life. That he *would not die, but live and declare the works of the Lord.* That is what I spoke around the house and I quickly corrected anyone else that said anything different, including him.

Hospice was now involved as well and at this time Ree's husband Daniel's Aunt Charlotte, who was very spiritual, came into the picture as Butch's personal *prayer warrior*. Thanks be to God for her, because He could not have sent a better person on assignment to him.

Aunt Charlotte kept in touch with Butch on a constant basis and continued to pray with him and to encourage him. She really inspired him, and from that, Butch started to really trust Aunt Charlotte with his deepest, darkest secrets. This included a past that had *haunted him* for decades. She, *by the grace of God*, helped him to find closure in this past, and out of that, prepared him for eternity as well.

Even though we were all believing in a miracle for his healing, one day Butch ran a sudden fever that did not break for a while.

He was still having *challenges* with breathing, but I had told him of a bible verse that spoke of *praising God even in your trials and tribulations*. So he was praising God all of the time during his episodes. He was also using natural herbs and *juicing* as well.

Someone who specialized in alternative medicine had suggested this technique. No one really understood why I would not give Butch regular foods, only natural juices, wheat grass, and other organic things.

We were spending a lot of money on herbs, organic vegetables, and such, for juicing, but we were willing to try whatever, no matter what. Anything was better than nothing right? It sure couldn't hurt him.

The Monday after Butch's episode with the fever, the volunteer from hospice informed me of Butch's grave condition. "Usually a high fever means that the patient will be gone soon. I'd give him possibly until the weekend to live."

"Well that's your opinion and I would rather that you keep it to yourself, because we are trying to stay *positive* in believing that God *will* heal him." I quickly corrected her and let her know that I did not want to hear this.

Within the next few days I drove up to see Aunt Charlotte. She advised, "Poo, I believe that Butch is giving up now. He has come to terms with it and he is now waiting to die."

"Oh no, Aunt Charlotte! What can we do about this?"

"Just keep talking to him and speaking positively. Let him know that we need him to keep fighting. If he gives up now, then we can no longer help him. He has to *believe* that he can beat this thing. Just try to let him know how important it is for him to *trust God* that he can survive."

Aunt Charlotte wanted me to continue to encourage Butch as she was attempting to do as well. But he was no longer hearing it.

Butch started to talk to Mommie, Poppie, his brothers, sisters, and everyone else about his demise. He apologized to everyone that he felt he had hurt over the years including Rose, who stayed by his side.

Butch continued to seek closure and continued to express how he had *found his peace with God*. He also spoke on the pending arrangements and how it should proceed.

"Poo, look, when I die, you and Ree save yourselves from all of the work of planning the funeral. I don't want you all to have to worry about anything."

I still did not want to hear it, so I kept *rebuking* what he was saying.

"Look, I rebuke all of that nonsense in Jesus' Mighty Name! You will not die, but live and declare the works of the Lord!" I proclaimed.

"Well you can rebuke it all you want to, but I am going to die!"

"I don't want to hear that!"

"Well just know it's going to happen, but I do not want you all to worry about anything." Butch kept saying.

I got tired of arguing and rebuking his words every time he spoke them. I also think that he got tired of me living in a *world of imagination* too, however he still did not push *the death subject* on me either.

People came to see him daily. All of his childhood friends, cousins, siblings, and Muddie stayed by his side constantly.

I really got tired of company because I wanted Butch all to our immediate family only. In all of my lifetime I had never had to come to grips with losing someone that I loved so deeply.

Sure I had lost other people that I truly cared for, even Dominique, but coping with my father being diagnosed with a terminal illness *cut me to the very core* of my being.

After all, I was Butch through and through, and coping with the realism of this was like *watching and feeling* my heart being *slowly* shred apart *day by day*. The torture was *utterly* unbearable!

Rose had gotten back on *crack* the year before, but she was even trying to be there for him. Butch tried to tell Rose that she needed to change. He continued to apologize to every one that he thought that he had hurt over the years as well.

He also had me to pay off all of his bills, which was very noble.

And then... Sunday morning came.

CHAPTER 43

At 6:59 A.M. this morning CoCo came to me, summoned by Butch. He was not breathing well at all, and he was trying to talk to me. "Poo, I am having a really hard time breathing." He labored as he spoke.

"Just relax, Butch. All is well. You just have to calm down." I replied.

"Can you call William for me?" he continued to agonize as he attempted to speak through the oxygen mask positioned over his nose.

"Okay, Butch, I will but you have to calm down! You're breathing very hard, and it doesn't help that you're trying to talk you know!" I said.

"William will call Ryan. How about Brea too?"

"Is she down here?" he asked.

"Yes."

"Well call her too," he said.

Butch seemed to know *more than I did* about this moment, but I did not question what he requested of me. I called William and Aunt Brea just as he asked me to.

"Please tell them to hurry up and come."

"Okay, Butch, I will. But you have got to stop talking right now! Save your strength, and hang in there."

In the meantime, I began to talk to him about staying positive. But this time he did not seem to be interested in what I was saying. He then proceeded to say, "I don't want to be a burden on you all."

And I replied, "You are not a burden on us, I am just a little tired right now."

I thought that he was talking about this particular morning that CoCo had woke me up. However, Butch was meaning for the *long-term*.

He seemed to have been pondering on this all morning because he was *so prepared* in what he was saying. I did not realize that he was beginning to say goodbye, but without alarming me.

By this time, Brea and my uncles William and Ryan began to walk into the house. Everyone felt what was happening. The fear and anxiety was apparent in everyone's eyes but *words were just left unspoken*.

As the morning progressed, Butch began to get uneasier and continued to struggle for breath. He was clearly more labored than ever. At this time I was highly concerned but still *moderately* calm. I was still quite oblivious to what was about to transpire.

Brea was trying to talk to him. "Butch, please just try to calm down. Try to relax. Just give it a moment. It'll get better."

I had him continue to settle down and practice breathing.

"Should I call Aunt Charlotte?" I asked him. As Butch nodded showing his approval, I was already dialing Aunt Charlotte's phone number. She had been getting ready for church.

"Hi, Charlotte, this is Poo… uh Butch is really having some problems breathing right now, and he wants to talk to you."

"Oh, my goodness, please put him on the phone," she said. As Charlotte began to pray with him over the phone, Butch attempted to raise his hands to praise God with what little strength he still had left.

I could hear Charlotte in the distance asking, "Butch, are you feeling any better?" She was trying to sooth him with a reassuring voice.

Butch continued to tell her nervously that he was still having some labor. "It's not getting any better."

"Okay, Butch who's in the room with you?" she asked him.

"Only Poo, Brea, William, and Ryan."

Then Aunt Charlotte asked to speak with Aunt Brea.

As I followed Brea out of the room, Aunt Charlotte continued to question her. "What is he doing now?" she asked.

Brea replied, "Nothing has changed."

"Okay, Brea, I want you to put everyone else out of the room, except for you and Poo! Just continue to pray until I get there. I am on my way, but let me speak to Poo first."

William and Ryan, both very nervous, walked out of the room for a quick cigarette break.

At this point I was silently following Brea down the hallway while she remained on the phone.

I continued to uneasily stare back at Butch, from down the hallway. As I looked back at him, his eyes were *solely* affixed on me. Our eyes met as if we were silently communicating. He was gazing expressionlessly at me, as though he was *giving his final farewell*.

As Brea passed the phone to me, Charlotte's words became *chilling* to say the least, "Poo, go back in there with your dad! The spirit of death is in the room with him! Go in there and do not stop praying with him until I get there! I am on the way!"

This was the only time that I had ever turned my eyes *or back* away from Butch and his constant stare of me. I tried to regain my composure, as anxiety struck me all over again.

As Brea and I silently entered the room, I suddenly realized that Butch's earlier gaze had been the last *soundless* communication between the two of us.

We made it *just in time* to see that Butch's eyes had closed, and his head had turned away from me.

His mouth was quickly gasping as though he was intensely sucking in the last breaths of air. Butch was beginning to go into *his death process*. As he took in his last gaping breath, Butch's body gently *thrusted* upwards.

"Please, Father, in the name of Jesus, don't take my daddy! Please don't take him from me! Please, please, Lord let him make it through this!"

I began to *continuously* rebuke the spirit of death and plead with God to save Butch. "Please Lord, I rebuke the spirit of death, and I plead the blood of Jesus over Butch that he is saved in Jesus' Mighty Name we pray." I kept repeating.

Brea though, on the other side of the room, was praying out as well. But I noticed that her prayer was suddenly changing. Before she had been praying the same way that I had been, but then after a short hesitation to look at Butch, Brea begin to speak again.

"Please, Lord, if this is your will, just help us to cope and please guide my brother safely into Your loving arms," I heard her saying from afar. Her prayer had become more of an *appeal* to God to help us to endure, instead of to save Butch.

For a moment I became *silently frustrated* with her, because I still wanted to believe that everything was going to be all right. At this point I was completely on top of Butch, pleading outwardly for God to spare his life.

"Please, God, help him!"

"Please save my dad!"

"Please don't let him die!"

As I cried aloud, I felt and heard the last gasps of air depart from his lungs as his body pulled forward one last time. Then everything went limp as silence stroked the air. I arose from over his body in a manner of utter disbelief and astonishment.

"So this was what death was really like?" I began to look out into a quiet gaze as I meditated on this question.

Understanding this was unlike any other experience that I had *ever* gone through. I had been through so much before, but *not in a lifetime*, would I have ever imagined this!

That gloomy August date will forever be *written upon my heart*. For this day, I will never forget when Butch passed away *right in my arms*.

CHAPTER 44

I suddenly kissed him on his forehead and said, "I could never kiss you when you were alive, but I am going to kiss my daddy now."

In the back of my mind, I recalled something that I had always heard, which was that the hearing was the last thing to leave in death. I did not know where that saying had come from, or if it was *even factual*, but at this point I began to howl out *emotionally* to Butch about how much I really did adore him. *Somehow he had to hear me*.

"I could never tell you how much I loved you, but you know I did! You were my daddy, and you were a good father to us! I love you so, so much! Butch, can you hear me? I want you to know this! I am so sorry for the things that happened between us! I really did love you! I apologize!" I screamed out as I continuously moaned with grief.

This was something that we still had not been able to tell each other, but we both knew it. After all, I was *him* all over, just in a female version. I was *Grace Marie*, which was the name that Muddie had chosen for Butch had he been a girl. I was that same person that Butch had always said, that he would have been had he been born female, which was *very wayward*.

My uncle William suddenly burst into the room with a mirror. "What is it? Oh no, Butch, say something, please," as he retrieved a mirror from the dresser nearby. He then put it up to Butch's nose.

William and Ryan had heard all of our wails, and they already knew what was happening.

"Butch, Butch… Butch, can you hear us? Say something if you can, please," Ryan continued to say.

At this time William was looking to see if any moisture would appear on the mirror.

"Call the time, Brea."

Aunt Brea was already calling the time, "Time of death, 9:04 A.M." This was his time of demise.

It was as if I was a world away from them and time had just *stopped*. I began to weep outwardly, but still openly praising God in the midst of my despair.

For a spell, Butch's death really tested my faith. Even though I was both wounded and feeling very let down with God *momentarily*, my mind reflected on the scripture that I had taught Butch about *praising God even in the midst of our tribulations*.

So I was obedient yet still reluctant to comprehend the reasoning behind this. As I cried, I still continued to pray and thank God for the time that we had Butch and let Him know just how grateful we were for Butch to have lived long enough to change his life.

My uncle Ryan came up from behind and began to embrace me, as he wept out as well. I was totally numb to him even holding me.

I knew then that there was no turning back for Butch. There had been nothing else for us to do except to accept the inevitable. I had just chosen not to.

I had instead chosen to rely on my faith, but I had to understand that this was not a *failure of my belief*. We are all born to die, and Butch was taken in God's time and not prematurely like he could have been.

Butch was going to die. However in his death, his life transformation allowed him to *yet live*. So actually that *gloomy* August day became a very celebratory occasion.

This date really was Butch's new date of eternal birth. For we must *all* go down the same passageway *once upon a time*. Does that make sense?

It is just up to us where we wish to spend eternity, up or down. *This is God's Holy Word.* Nevertheless, I began to ponder on Butch's death.

Although soon afterwards, I began to realize, "How could I have actually rebuked the will of God, when He has *all power*?" For God's will is yet perfect, and I truly believe that *He* came to claim Butch's soul.

He had died honoring God, and it became *the most amazing thing* that I had *ever* experienced in my life. If death could be beautiful, Butch's finality had been *utterly astonishing*.

It is *truly* hard to cope with death. The magnitude and the permanence are certainly difficult, but we must realize that it is still a part of life. It is something that we *all* must experience to have eternal life. The uncertainty is quite scary at times, but *we must all prepare* for it.

And how beautiful is the death of one of God's saints? Yes, death too can be beautiful depending on the circumstances. This may not make full sense unless you have had a chance to experience someone dying like this.

Aunt Charlotte suddenly ran into the house. By this time of course, it was already too late and she knew it.

We exchanged visual expressions that both posed the question and gave her the answer that she *ultimately* did not want to hear but somehow already knew.

"Oh, Poo, no! I already felt that but I didn't want to believe it! I hit every red light between my house and here!" Charlotte exclaimed. Well I guess I wasn't supposed to make it here in time, huh?"

I never responded as she started for the hallway to enter the bedroom where Butch's body lay totally lifeless. As she entered the threshold of the room Charlotte closed the door behind her.

As I stood there still *semi-motionless*, I could hear her as she was closing the door, speaking directly to Butch. "Well, you went on and left us, huh, Butch?"

For she too had lost a very dear friend that she had grown very fond of.

It seemed to take forever for the funeral home to come to get his body, but this also allowed for a lot of our family members to come to view him lying in state as well. It now seemed like family had *come out of the woodwork* just to see Butch before the hearse came to retrieve his body.

It just all seemed so *surreal* for someone who had once lived his life to the fullest. It just seemed *all too hard* to associate Butch with the word *death*. But I guess that is true with any loved one's death.

Butch had been no different than anyone else's father, mother, sibling, friend, or other loved one that had passed away. He was no more special than anyone else. But he *WAS* my daddy and I suddenly missed him *so* much.

I will never forget how my cousin's husband, Red, tried to console me as the mortician came to retrieve Butch's body from the house. No matter how hard he tried to shield me, I had to see my daddy being rolled away on the stretcher with that sheet draped over his body. I had to see him being lifted into the hearse. After all, this was my confirmation to the unimaginable. I had to see it all!

Standing on my porch, my mind drifted a million miles away. Suddenly Uncle William walked up beside me to talk. "Poo, don't worry about anything. We have it all under control. We'll take care of everything."

I never replied as my eyes continued to stroke the far distance. In my grief and despair, I had heard everything Uncle William had said to me. Even in my dismay, my soul was *suddenly* engulfed with an everlasting flame of anger.

Who in the hell were these people? My family, the same one that had always belittled us and thought less of us, was now trying to tell us that they would take over. No one ever gave Ree and me any credit, but Butch's family would not have *the last say so*. Not this time! Not in my daddy's funeral planning. After all, Butch belonged to God *and then to us*. Not to them! And I was not little weak Rose! Remember I was the bold, outspoken one that Mommie and Muddie both had a hand in shaping. So I was not going to just *roll over and play dead*.

As Uncle William walked away, I then heard a soothing voice *whisper into my ear*, "The book is finished." Just as fast as the rage had newly anchored, the peace of God subtly came in to erase it all as a single tear streamed from my eye.

My mouth flew open, as I gasped openly. "The book was about Butch, not about me! Oh my God!" Revelation had just come into my spirit *and instantly* I felt that the book that I had been longing to write was suddenly completed. In that instance I visualized a book suddenly closing shut, and I then knew that Butch's life had been the story that God had given to me to write all along.

As I continued to blankly stare, I felt Red grab me by the arm. "Come on, Poo."

As he led me down the street, away from all of the confusion it actually made it easier for me to see it all.

My legs began to quiver beneath me as the hearse drove slowly alongside of us. No, this just could not be my dad in the back! We had just been talking to one another a couple of hours before and now this! Every second, every minute that passed afterward seemed as if *a lifetime* had already passed by.

I had not heard Butch's voice in a few hours, however I *now knew* that it would be another lifetime until we could possibly speak again, *except for maybe in my dreams*.

Death was now permanent, and forever was now reality. It was all just too hard to understand, and *somehow* part of a *new chapter* in my life that was just beginning. Love it or hate it, I now had to deal with it. There was no other option. Butch was gone, and we could not bring him back.

I had been blessed with Butch for nearly twenty-seven years of my life, but I selfishly still wanted more. It was not enough, *but it was what it was*. It was still God's gift to us either way.

Butch could have been gone so many times before when he was living his life *on the edge*. He could have been killed when he was not prepared to die, so God was merciful on his life. We just had to recognize this and be grateful for the time that we did have with him, but that *is always* easier said than done.

CHAPTER 45

The afternoon of Butch's death everyone left Ree, CoCo, and me alone. Everyone gathered in *other places* to discuss the pending arrangements. But we were his daughters and *no one* had the right to do anything without us.

All we had was each other. We did not even have Rose, who had come and gone, and was probably somewhere trying to get as high as she could get just to deal with Butch's loss.

Everyone had always counted us down. After all, we had come from parents that had messed up all of their lives, so what had made us any better? That was according to everyone else anyway, but they just did not know that because of our constant struggles, we had more *fight* in us than they wanted to deal with. And *Poo* was definitely *geared up* to go the distance, if that is what it took.

As we all know, whenever *money* is involved, most of the time there is going to be tension and Butch's death had been no different. Arguments over who was going to take the lead had brought on a brief dispute between our uncles, aunts, grandmother, and us, but I could care less what someone else had thought.

There was no way in hell that I was going to back out of this one. My family had no choice but to respect Ree and I, and our wish for Butch's funeral and that is what they did. I was the oldest and I took over immediately. Then God blessed us with everything in the right place, at the right time.

As the day progressed, Butch's cousin, Roland, came by to give us his condolences. Since we had never done this before, Roland started our *creative juices to flowing*. He knew that we were definitely determined to plan this funeral right, regardless of the *obstacles* in our way. Roland gave Ree and I an idea of what we needed to work on to plan the funeral. "What about the venue? What about the cemetery plot? Do you have all of that taken care of?"

"Yes, we do." Ree and I both exclaimed.

"Okay what about the date, the flowers, the soloist, and so on?"

By this time Ree was writing down everything that he was telling us. As Roland continued to tell us what we needed to take care of this funeral planning, we realized that God was directing our path through him.

"Now do not worry about the food, because I already have that taken care of, at no cost."

"Oh thank you, Roland! That is wonderful!" I said.

He owned a few businesses, one of which was a catering service and that came in very handy for us. So the food was already taken care of, free of charge.

Butch's niece Jackie also would let us use her house for the repass because she had a large open backyard area. God was just putting everything in order for us.

Then in walked Rose's cousin, Sandy, who had sang semi-professionally. So Sandy became our soloist for the ceremony.

Even Ree's husband, Daniel, was involved in helping out with the preparations as well. His father was the captain at the county sheriff's department, so the escorting was already covered too.

Ree and I would purchase all of the flowers and sprays; we already had Butch's suit picked out, so that was done; and I had access to all of his military records and discharge papers as well. So everything just seemed to be falling into place.

The day that we met at the funeral home with Butch's siblings and other family to discuss everything, we already had it all taken care of. They seemed to be so astonished at the fact that we did not need them. We were just as good as our family was, and they had to know that *we had our own voice*.

Butch, next to God, belonged to us not to them. He was *OUR* dad. Just because our parents had not always made wise choices did not mean that we were any less than anyone else.

Roland said that Ree and I were some *really bad girls* when it came to brains. But we already knew that, and were just about to show everyone else just how *smart* we truly were. We already knew what it took to survive because we were survivors.

So no decisions could or would be made on our behalf. Our *stamp of approval* was on everything. We were *going to be* in control, and for that I stood my ground, despite my family's objections.

Everything had been so busy that week that Ree and I did not get much time to grieve. We were at Mommie and Poppie's constantly, either discussing the plans, talking about how our family was treating us, writing the obituary for the local newspaper, or designing the programs.

Everything was just flowing so perfectly that we already knew God had to be *in the mix* on this one.

We already had Butch's suit for the interment, so I took that to the funeral home. However the mortician also instructed me to buy new undergarments for him as well; even though Butch already had *clean* underwear and such, he still said that they needed to be *brand new*. Now I had a problem with buying a new t-shirt, socks, and underwear for a *dead body*, and I did not understand it, but I did it anyway. It all seemed so strange, but every detail had to be taken care of leading up to that dreary day of the service.

We were still having problems getting a barber to come out to cut Butch's hair so Jerry *did the honors* for us. He and brother-in-law Daniel went to the funeral home to prepare Butch's hair and face.

When they returned home, Daniel seemed rather *freaked out* because Jerry had been talking to Butch as though he were still alive. It did seem *rather strange*, but we were all dealing with this preparation in different ways.

This actually had been a good thing for Jerry, because he really needed that closure as well. His own dad had passed away when he was sixteen, and Butch had become a *surrogate father* to him over the years. They really had a *strong bond* between the two of them. They had even traveled back and forth to Chicago together frequently. Jerry and Butch traveled so regularly together that his friends and family began to call him *Cousin Butch*.

Since I was such a *nag* on trips, Butch would only go if I was not going. He would say, "Is Poo going? If so, I am not going." Butch always wanted to *party* once he got there, and that he did very well. When I would go, I would constantly try to keep Butch in line, but that was *next to impossible*.

One time Jerry and I had come up on his brother and Butch standing around a local liquor store just drinking and *hanging out* with friends. This was *the norm* back then so it was not really anything *out of the ordinary*.

We had driven up and stopped to talk to them. When all of a sudden, Chicago police came upon the scene to clear the premises. Butch quickly tried to pass his open bottle of beer to me, but I did not want to take it. He was anxiously saying, "Here, girl! Take this!" Then I said, "No, I am not taking that!" Then he responded, "Girl, take this! I ain't even supposed to be out of the state of Texas. You know I am still on probation," as he passed it to me anyway.

He had been placed on probation for a prior cocaine possession charge that had made him begin to *change his life for the better*. I did say *for the better*, but still not *all of the way*.

Butch had always *still been Butch*, and because of that relationship, Jerry really did love him. He adored him just as much as we did, and it was utterly apparent in the way that he assisted Butch before he passed away. So this was a great thing for Jerry to talk it out.

CHAPTER 46

Approaching the morning of the service, the clock continued to tick leisurely but certainly, as I was consumed with total anxiety. I wanted everything to be perfect, and so far it had been.

We had already viewed Butch's body the day before and the wake had transpired that night before also. Rose had even decided to check herself into a rehabilitation facility for her drug addiction that day as well. It seemed like we had nothing else to worry about, other than the scheduled service itself.

I had even made peace with Butch's *other woman*, Stella, who had been the object of his affection at the time when Rose left us. Stella had already attempted to reach out to me at Muddie's house, but I would not respond to her. I had carried a grudge against her for tearing our family apart in those earlier years. How wrong was I to be this way?

My cousin Jackie watched as I left Muddie's house to confront Stella.

I went out to be mean but instead my words *spit out* with total forgiveness. "Stella, we need to talk." "What's on your mind, Poo?" "Are you coming to Butch's funeral tomorrow?" "I had planned to, why?"

"Well I am sorry for being mean to you yesterday at the house. I do realize that Butch did love you and maybe you loved him also. I did hold a grudge against you, but *who am I to judge you*? I have also messed around, even with married men as well. So I am no better than you. I just wanted you to know that I forgive you and I know that Butch would want you with his family. So please make sure to come for the services."

Instant relief and complete astonishment then filled Stella's face, as she leaned over to hug me. How could I hold this against her, when I myself had subsequently dated a married man and felt that I had loved him also? *I was no better than she was.*

For relationships, I have found, are all too easy to get entangled in whether good or bad. So I could not hold her to any higher standard than I held myself; therefore, I expressed my forgiveness to her and asked for the same. Afterward we embraced once again and I knew that Butch would have been *thrilled* with that. For he did still love Stella and was only *going it solo* because he wanted to please Ree, CoCo, and me. But he still talked to her as often as he could also. After all, Rose was still with our stepfather, Allen, who was having a really hard time dealing with her crack usage. They had been together for about five years now and Allen had been *coping* with Rose's drug abuse, as he dealt with his own *alcoholic demons* too. Even so, he and Butch had always been *cordial*, so Allen was right there by our sides as well.

Butch had touched him also, as he had come home one morning wearing Allen's raincoat and riding his bicycle. I looked at Jerry, *too scared* to say anything, as Jerry looked on *in astonishment* and with a *questionable* smile upon his face. "Why in the hell are you wearing Allen's raincoat and riding his bike?" I said to Butch.

"Oh, he let me use it," he said with a smile.

"Let me call Rose and see what is going on?" I announced as I picked up the phone to call her.

"Hello, Rose?"

"Hey, Poo!"

"Yes, Rose, why is Butch wearing Allen's jacket and riding his bike?"

Rose began to laugh as I inquired further.

"No, Rose, stop playing! What's going on?"

"Let Butch tell you."

"No I am asking you."

"Okay, he got caught up with some old woman that cheated him out of his money and he came over here to talk to us. Then it began to rain so he spent the night over here."

"With you and Allen?"

"Yes, girl, with both of us! But don't tell him that I told you everything. Okay?"

"Alright, I won't. As long as everything is okay, because we thought that he had done something to Allen or something." I replied with relief.

"No, he was just caught up *messing around*."

"That's terrible, but I am glad that everything is okay."

"Yeah it's fine."

"Alright, Rose, we will talk to you later. Bye! Love you!"

"Yeah, love you too, Poo."

So Butch had touched everyone with his *unique brand* of comedic outreach.

Allen was now with Butch's wife, because Rose and he were still married when he passed, but Butch was fine with this *arrangement* as it was.

Rose and Butch truly demonstrated *a special kind of love* for one another. This *love* had surpassed twenty-nine years *of all understanding* when he died, and Rose really did take it hard.

CHAPTER 47

The morning of the service, we were greeted with the programs that we had arranged as we all got into the family car. They had come out so well except for a couple of misplaced words that I noticed almost immediately. But still there were no complaints. We were all so relieved to see the fruits of our labor and it was just the way Ree and I had envisioned it.

Driving to the church had been a piece of cake. We were still in amazement over the programs and just how excellent everything had come together over the past week.

As we approached the church, two long black hearses stationed outside cheerlessly welcomed us. At this time my stomach began to *tie into knots*, for this was the day that we would never see Butch again.

Even though he had died, we still had his body to view. But after today, I knew that his remains would also be gone forever. As I entered the foyer of the church, I began to experience the heartache of another elongated walk up to a coffin of a loved one that had left us way too soon.

As the assembly of mourners rose when we entered into the sanctuary, dancing visions of dismal faces silently met my tear-stained eyes. At that moment they were all just *faces in a familiar crowd* of extended friends and family. I really could not focus on anyone.

My only thoughts were on Butch who was laid there on his back. My dad, the father whom I would never hear crack another joke, or curse me out when I had messed up.

As I neared his casket, my knees began to buckle and quiver. I could no longer feel my legs beneath me, as I began to wail. Abruptly reality started to hit me. *Why couldn't this all just be a dream?*

Upon approach, I leaned over Butch's corpse and began to stroke his head. I had been the only one who was *poised* all week, even at the wake. I had been the only one that had not really cried openly.

Everybody had been concerned about *Poo*.

"Are you okay?"

"What about Poo? How is she taking it?" Everyone had wondered, even though I *continuously* assured them that I was fine. "Seriously, I will be alright," I kept saying to everyone.

All week there had been too many things to do to cry. Someone had to take care of the *business at hand*. But suddenly the time had neared to stop and finally cope with it, and now even *Poo* was beginning to fold.

The sudden comprehension that Butch was gone from our lives for good hurt me more than the *very essence* of pain itself. I just could not bear the thought of it any longer. It was all too much to manage at one time. He had been the only one *true* stable parent that we had over the years. Rose had been *up and down*, and now he was gone for eternity.

Why? Why couldn't he have beaten this thing? Why him? I began to speak erratically into Butch's ear, as though he could hear me, "No more pain, no more suffering, Butch! It's all gone."

At this point Jerry was pulling me away from the casket and attempting to sit me down. I was *deeply distraught*, and it did take a few moments, but once I began to focus again on reality, much to my surprise, one of my coworkers' faces became visible in my sight. She had come up to help Jerry with me, as she sorrowfully embraced me at the coffin.

I already knew that Theresa was there, because she had kissed my cheek earlier at the house. She had also become very familiar with Butch over the years. But one by one, I realized that several of my other coworkers *and friends* were in attendance as well. That included my immediate supervisor and that seemed to immediately lift my spirits.

It seemed that my local office had allowed everyone that had wanted to come to Butch's funeral time off to support me, and I was very grateful for that. Everyone had known the hard life that I had once lived, and they knew just how important my dad had been to me. So to see them there made me feel both loved and supported for the moment. From that point on, I knew that everything would be okay.

When the time came for remarks, the minister began to call for everyone who wanted to speak and, much to the surprise of everyone else; I was the first to arise.

Keep in mind; I always possessed that certain *charisma* from childhood, so it was always quite natural to take the lead *wherever* I was without hesitation.

I had to let everyone know what God had done for Butch, and how *God's grace and mercy* had truly changed his life around. I spoke of how he had died *praising God*, which was a distant cry from the person that most had grown accustomed to. Then I had to inform them on just how *beautiful* Butch's death had been, despite his former shortcomings. I also wanted the gathering to know just how important and loved Butch was. To the critics, I advised that *no sin was greater than another*, except for one, and I urged them to adjust what they may need to change in their own lives.

After this, one by one, people began to follow to speak of *the good times* that they had with Butch and just how he had touched their lives in some form or fashion. With that, the memorial service proceeded very nicely.

The theme gradually became *God's splendid grace* operating in Butch's life. Everything was focused on just how he had altered his life for the better.

Then Sandy sang so melodiously as she belted out *Amazing Grace*.

It really became *the celebration of life* that I had so emphasized upon in the program, and it really set the tone for happiness, not sadness. It was more upbeat than most memorials that I had subsequently attended, and the preacher continued upon the subject of *joy in the death of one of God's saints*.

Because of the tone, it was like *a weight had instantly been taken off of my shoulders*. We had been successful in our planning and may have even *saved some souls* along the way as well.

After the service, we lined up in the procession behind the two hearses. One carried Butch's body, and the other *filled* with flowers and sprays. There were also two family cars. One carried Ree's and my families, and the other carried Muddie and Butch's siblings.

There was still some *conflict* between our family and us because it was *evident* that they could not control us. But who really cared at this point anyway. Our goals had been met and that is all that we had ever wanted.

We watched in admiration, as everything became obvious of just how cherished Butch really had been. From the family car we observed the numerous cars that followed silently behind. The procession wrapped around a bend in the path along the expressway. It seemed to be a few miles long, as Ree's father-in-law and fellow coworkers escorted us to the cemetery. Even though Butch had lived his life as a *mere man*, he was buried *with the dignity of a king*.

At the site, I received the American flag for Rose for his tenure in the Air Force.

In the distance, someone in the mass began to sing, *When the Saints Go Marching In*.

It was all very nice, but I was *so* happy for the day to finally come to an end. Now we could have the time to properly grieve as we needed to, and that we did.

CHAPTER 48

A few months after Butch's death, Ree graduated from nursing school, *in spite of* the problems that her and Daniel were starting to have.

This had been the day that Butch was determined to see and we were all *very excited* for her, because *this was a very huge milestone*.

We all knew at this point, she could be successful in whatever she strived to do with or without her husband.

The morning of her graduation was one of bittersweet memory. It was very happy, yet sad as well. Ree and I both understood that we were truly *all that we had*, and that was quite painful. We had no mother to stand beside us because Rose was still off on crack, and Butch was now gone.

We also realized that it was *totally* up to us to *make the most* of the celebration, and that we did.

I put Ree's picture in the local newspaper to announce her accomplishment along with the phrase, "Congratulations, sister! Butch would have been proud!"

That morning we got up with the sunrise to *steal* Mommie and Poppie's newspaper, since they lived right down the street from us, and the paper was *just lying there*. As we unfolded their paper, giggling about what we were doing, Ree said, "Poo, I cannot believe that this is actually happening! All of my hard work has finally paid off! Can you believe it?"

Elatedly I said, "Yeah, for all of the people that counted us down. They just didn't know that we were some *bad bitches*, did they!"

Then Ree's smile perked up as she replied, "Girl, you and that dirty mouth! You need to pray for God to take that away from you!"

"Whatever! You know that you love me, girl! And God still loves me too, *despite* my *bad* ways. But for the record, I am praying for Him to *deliver* me from this bad mouth too!" jokingly I added.

As the day progressed and we all prepared to go to the commencement, it seemed as though everyone was moving *at a snail's pace*. Finally we arrived, just in time to sit with all of my aunts, uncles, and cousins from both sides of our family. Everyone had come out in support of Ree and her efforts and everyone was quite proud of her accomplishment.

As she walked across the stage to receive her Bachelor's degree I rose proudly for my sister, clapping wildly and openly beaming. It all just seemed so surreal and slow motioned.

Out of all of us, Ree had never fallen short of her dream to finish college, despite having a child and a failing marriage. She also knew that out of everyone in that audience, I was the most proud.

My mind quickly recalled visions of the little sandy haired girl with the big hazel eyes running up behind me to the screen of our old *shotgun house* to ask, "Whatcha doing, Rose?"

I thought of all of the people that I had bullied as a child, to keep them from picking on her back in the day. Then I remembered how I had tried to teach her how to read, and she would cry out hysterically and say, "I can't!" Then I would get mad and call her a *dummy*.

I also recollected the time that the children's service was about to place us in foster care after Rose had abandoned us, and Ree cried because she thought that we would be split up. I angrily told her, "You know my name, and I know yours! So we can look each other up later if that happens! Besides you'll probably get adopted anyway, because you're light-skinned. I will probably have to stay in foster care until I'm grown, because no one will want me! Just quit crying like a damn baby!"

Inside I was just as scared as she was. I wanted to cry too, fighting back my tears all of the way. But I knew that I had to be the strong one. *I always did.* I had to keep my composure as the big sister who somehow had all of the right answers. At least growing up, Ree always thought so anyway.

No one really understood the bond that we shared. No matter what the problem was, Ree and I always stuck together. We went through the good and the bad, throughout all of the battles and all of the love, *together*.

I was *the crazy one* that everyone knew would take care of the problem, however *unorthodox* it was. Ree was *the peacemaker*, who tried to avoid conflict, but would still riot up whenever necessary. We were still part of the same team, *Poo and Ree*, and she knew that I loved her for that.

As I stood there clapping among my family I suddenly looked over my shoulder. It was as if I could feel Butch's presence there with us. He had finally seen all that he needed to see, and that was *his girls*, who would finally be okay without him there.

You know it is really bad when everyone around you counts you down. They just do not realize that it is *not always a given* that just because your parents do not achieve, that it automatically means that you are a failure.

Thanks be to God, that He *is* a God of the underdog and I believe that He honored every prayer that Butch had requested of Him. *How good to finally be on the receiving end.*

Soon after Ree graduated from college, things really started to *look up* for us.

God *completely* delivered Rose from the crack addiction, so she was *finally* back in our lives.

Then CoCo grew up and started her own family. Her books, *The L-O-V-E Trilogies*, should be coming soon.

Then Ree and I moved closer to one another in homes that we could only imagine about.

Now I did not finish college after all, but my job at the airlines became even better than it was before.

Everything was in a steady upward flow. I had gone from making moderate money to *topping out* over fifty thousand a year, without a degree. *So I was not hurting either*.

Everything that Butch had dreamt for us was suddenly coming to pass. Everyone that had counted us down could only take notice to what God was openly doing for us.

"Hey girl, what are you all doing over there today?" I hollered at Ree from across the street, with a big gloating smile, as she replied back with an equal gleam.

"Nothing girl, just trying to get it all together! You know!" Her house and landscape so magnificently decorated just the way that she liked it.

Walking back into my own home, all I could do was marvel over the way things had been unfolding. God had *exceedingly and abundantly* blessed us with homes customized just as we desired and dreamed them to be; Ree's with an elegant design that highlighted a graceful full formal stairwell, built with the look of a small mansion; and mine, focused on family, with an extremely large kitchen and den area for all of those *pre-holiday* cooking parties with our entire family.

God was blessing us *openly* just as He does for so many others. For these same little girls that had been through so much and who had endured such hard times before, we were finally *on top of our game*. Butch's prayers all seemed to have been answered, for we had finally made it *out of the struggle*.

"Can you believe this, Jerry? Look how God has blessed us all," I exclaimed as we lay on the floor looking up at the vaulted ceiling of our new two-story dwelling. *It is still so hard to believe*. Whoever knew that we could accomplish just what we set out to do?

And me... *I began to write again also*. This time I will not stop short of my goals. And *the sky is the limit* from there.

You know what they always say, "When life gives you lemons, you make lemonade." Now you figure it out from there.

Just stay on the right pathway and even if you *venture off* a little, please do not *ever* give up on your dreams. Remember that the best is *still* yet to come! *To be continued...*

The _Ending_: "No Turning Back..."

This book was truly meant to be. It was truly *my destiny*. Even though I could never adore God as much as He has *impartially* loved me throughout the years, I commit to certainly strive to do so, for the rest of my lifetime.

For He has significantly blessed me with an absolutely sacred testimony that someone (*hopefully*) will both understand and utterly appreciate, and for that I am truly thankful!

I had always possessed an internal *motherly nurture* for Rose and Butch. When they could not do it for themselves, I always tried my greatest to step in and assist them, whatever the circumstance, and this is where I continuously battled God for control. I thought that I could handle things by myself, instead of *letting go and letting God* take care of it. I had to *always* be in charge.

But where is God's glory in man interfering? God can handle it *all by Himself* and *He* definitely does not have to share the glory with anyone else.

He is God all by Himself, and finally, after many years of struggle, I think that I have faithfully passed this test. *To God be all of the glory!*

You know, no one has a choice in who their parents are, or in how they will look, or in what talents they may or may not possess. These are all the special characteristics that make up your individual life and ultimately the beginnings of your own individual testimony. *Who are you and whom do you belong to?* As for me, I *solemnly* belong to God...

Even though this tumultuous journey has been filled with its various *peaks and valleys,* through it all these *life's lessons* have all been unified to guide my feet onto the right pathway that God has desired of me to go.

Everyone goes through *struggles of sort.* Life in itself is a constant battle contrasted between right, wrong, good and bad. Everyone has a story to tell, a purpose, a destiny in life. It is just up to each one of us to recognize our own individual niche and to understand just what it is that God has *laid upon our hearts* to do.

For me, it has taken a span of fourteen years to totally discover who I really was and to truly know in which direction my life was actually going. The ride has been quite bumpy at times too.

For every comfort that I have had over the years has *subtly* been taken away from me, yet in seasons. When reminiscing upon the past it seems *awfully hard* to fathom just how I was able to continue to motivate myself over and over to stay focused.

I must give it *all* to God, my Heavenly Father, who has continuously comforted and kept me through all of the *laughter*, the *pain*, and the *raindrops*.

Thanks be to Him, for loving and birthing this vision within me. I spoke it and believed that this dream would be manifested, and God, You so awesomely blessed it, and for all of that I am truly grateful.

Thank You for all of *life's characters* that I have encountered upon this earthly expedition.

Thank You God *most of all* for my family and the *circle of friends* that you have encompassed me with over the years.

To those who inspired me along the way, *I give you many thanks*.

To my children; God you knew just what I needed to slow me down. *SMILE!*

And to Jerry... *My*, I once heard it said somewhere that you should have someone in your life that is at least willing to go *down the middle of the road* with you, and Jerry has *in fact* been that someone. I never deserved him, but I am *greatly* appreciative for who God has blessed me with.

Growing up together, I now realize that Jerry and I compliment each other. Where he is weak, I am strong, and where I am weak, he is strong. He is my support.

He came from a larger family than I did; however, we both grew up rather poor, yet joyful. Struggle is what we both understood, and we could share with each other because of it.

There are *so many* similarities between us, *but* varied differences as well.

Over the years we have weathered some really excruciating storms *together*. Nevertheless, we have also experienced some of the *greatest of times* within our battles as well, if that makes sense. Remember, the challenges will either compel you to become closer bonded or divide you farther apart.

You must also live with the faith and knowledge that *God can and will* change your cloudy days, *regardless of what they are*, and *prayer* will also bring you closer together too.

Remember, with God, you *are* the majority and not the minority. All you need is a word to stand on, and *it shall come to pass*. We have seen the miraculous results for ourselves.

For there have been numerous times that Jerry and I have stood in *agreement* for things, and watched God *show up* and *show out*.

How awesome is it to find real love? How even greater is it to find peace in God?

With the closing of this book, I have finally found the *serenity* and *finality* that I had been seeking *all* of my life. Since I was that little girl growing up, looking for love in *all* of the wrong places, dealing with low self-esteem, self-hatred, self-doubt, disappointment, and grief. I never felt that I was *worthy enough* to be content, *but God somehow knew better.*

In *finding myself* over the years, I realize that all of the *raindrops* have actually been *stepping-stones* to my own personal triumph and victory. These same *tear-stained crosses to bear* have actually become my crossroads, to allow me to discover the solace within. They have truly made me the woman that I am today.

For all of the *laughter* and the *raindrops*… Thank You God!

If I had it all over to do again, I would have it no other way. For this is my personal life's story. This role was made *especially* for me, from the very time of my creation. This is sincerely who I am. *I am a survivor!* I have overcome all of the strife that has constantly embattled me along the way, and I *thank You* Father for that.

For You have made my life special *just for me!*

Again thank You God for the ride. *"It's been real…"*

Sincerely,
C. L. Gray

C. L. Gray is both a wife and mother of four. Retired from Southwest Airlines, she has begun her lifetime aspiration of becoming a full time novelist. As the author of *From Dirt to DESTINY*, she has evolved on the scene, to display an appealing versatility with her various writing styles. This also includes her latest creation, a romance novel, ingeniously titled, *Nostalgia: A Journey Through Love,* coming soon. Look for more of her works in the near future.